The Industrial Revolution

A History in Documents

The Industrial Revolution

A History in Documents

Laura L. Frader

OXFORD
UNIVERSITY PRESS

OXFORD
UNIVERSITY PRESS

Oxford University Press, Inc., publishes works that further
Oxford University's objective of excellence
in research, scholarship, and education.

Oxford   New York
Auckland Cape Town Dar es Salaam Hong Kong Karachi
Kuala Lumpur Madrid Melbourne Mexico City Nairobi
New Delhi Shanghai Taipei Toronto

With offices in
Argentina Austria Brazil Chile Czech Republic France Greece
Guatemala Hungary Italy Japan Poland Portugal Singapore
South Korea Switzerland Thailand Turkey Ukraine Vietnam

Copyright © 2006 by Laura L. Frader

Published by Oxford University Press, Inc.
198 Madison Avenue, New York, New York 10016
www.oup.com

Oxford is a registered trademark of Oxford University Press

Library of Congress Cataloging-in-Publication Data
Frader, Laura Levine
The industrial revolution : a history in documents / Laura L. Frader.
p. cm.
Includes index.
ISBN-13: 978-0-19-512817-8
ISBN-10: 0-19-512817-6
1. Industrial revolution—Sources. 2. Industrialization—History. I. Title.
HD2329.F73 2005
330.9'034—dc22
2005015167

Printed in the United States of America on acid-free paper

Cover: *Coal mines and clay
quarries in France, 19th century*

Frontispiece: *Workers at a
Danish steel mill, 1885*

Title page: *The Krupp steel
works in Essen, Germany, 1912*

Contents

What Is a Document?

To the historian, a document is, quite simply, any sort of historical evidence. It is a primary source, the raw material of history. A document may be more than the expected government paperwork, such as a treaty or passport. It is also a letter, diary, will, grocery list, newspaper article, recipe, memoir, oral history, school yearbook, map, chart, architectural plan, poster, musical score, play script, novel, political cartoon, painting, photograph—even an object.

Using primary sources allows us not just to read *about* history, but to read history itself. It allows us to immerse ourselves in the look and feel of an era gone by, to understand its people and their language, whether verbal or visual. And it allows us to take an active, hands-on role in (re)constructing history.

Using primary sources requires us to use our powers of detection to ferret out the relevant facts and to draw conclusions from them; just as Agatha Christie uses the scores in a bridge game to determine the identity of a murderer, the historian uses facts from a variety of sources—some, perhaps, seemingly inconsequential—to build a historical case.

The poet W. H. Auden wrote that history was the study of questions. Primary sources force us to ask questions—and then, by answering them, to construct a narrative or an argument that makes sense to us. Moreover, as we draw on the many sources from "the dust-bin of history," we can endow that narrative with character, personality, and texture—all the elements that make history so endlessly intriguing.

Cartoon
This political cartoon addresses the issue of church and state. It illustrates the Supreme Court's role in balancing the demands of the 1st Amendment of the Constitution and the desires of the religious population.

Illustration
Illustrations from children's books, such as this alphabet from the New England Primer, tell us how children were educated, and also what the religious and moral values of the time were.

Map
A 1788 British map of India shows the region prior to British colonization, an indication of the kingdoms and provinces whose ethnic divisions would resurface later in India's history.

Treaty
A government document such as this 1805 treaty can reveal not only the details of government policy, but information about the people who signed it. Here, the Indians' names were written in English transliteration by U.S. officials; the Indians added pictographs to the right of their names.

Literature
The first written version of the Old English epic Beowulf, from the late 10th century, is physical evidence of the transition from oral to written history. Charred by fire, it is also a physical record of the wear and tear of history.

How to Read a Document

By the time of the industrial revolution, print technology had evolved to the point where engravings, posters, photographs, and broadsides—printed sheets that were often given away or sold for a penny a piece—could be mechanically reproduced and widely distributed. Some artists painted pictures of industrial achievements; others turned their cameras' lenses on the cramped and unhealthy conditions in which industrial workers lived and labored. Patents document new inventions; government reports on factory conditions and work accidents provide a window into the lives of ordinary working people. Political tracts, poetry, novels, sheet music, advice books, and even cookbooks are other important sources of information about the lives of the middle and working classes and the political movements that emerged during the industrial revolution.

Reading and making sense of these historical documents requires a critical eye. Some factors to consider are when and why the document was produced, who produced it, and what that person's political views might have been. Being aware of the context in which the author wrote the document is important to understanding the meaning of what they wrote. To whom was the document addressed and how did it attempt to communicate a particular message? How might the document have been used by its audience?

The accident report and the poster on the opposite page both reflect concerns about industrial conditions, but they were directed at very different audiences. The factory inspector who wrote the report generated a record for the government, simply reporting what happened. The poster issued a call to workers to support a strike, and was destined to be posted on lampposts or the sides of buildings in a working-class neighborhood to attract the attention of passers-by.

Context

A British factory inspector wrote this report on a work accident in 1859. By this time, the British government was investigating the employers' employment and treatment of children and young persons working in factories. Although factory legislation limited child labor, children older than twelve were still permitted to work up to ten hours a day.

Format and Content

The document is a form that was filled out by the factory inspector. It reports the name and age of the worker who suffered the accident, the nature of the accident, and the place and date it occurred. It also provides the victim's own description of the accident, how she was overcome by "giddiness" when her hand slipped into the mechanism of a steam-driven ("self-acting") spinning machine ("mule"). The language of the report suggests that the inspector transcribed the worker's testimony directly, without including his own opinion.

Interpretation

To interpret this kind of formal report it is important to read between the lines. Although it is intended to be objective, the report can still reveal much about the lives of adolescent girls. For example, when the girl said that she had been overcome by "giddiness," perhaps she was tired from working such long hours. The inspector focused on the worker's momentary lapse, rather than point to the absence of safety equipment on the machine.

Audience

In contrast to the factory inspector's report, this document is intended for a broader public audience and has a specific point of view. The poster is addressed to "fellow workers," conveying a sense of fraternity between the authors and the audience. And it is an appeal to both "tailors and tailoresses," suggesting the labor movement involved both men and women.

Context

Labor activists belonging to the tailors' union printed this poster at the time of the 1889 London tailors' strike. Tailors, like many other workers in Britain, were agitating for better working conditions and higher wages.

Format and Content

Labor activists used posters such as this one, which was probably displayed on walls or lamp-posts in a working-class district of London, to attract the attention of workers and encourage them to mobilize. They also served to educate workers—and the public at large—about workers' rights. This poster states the reasons for the strike, lists the strike demands, and appeals to workers to quit work by the day of the strike. The "sweaters" mentioned in the poster are workers who were paid by the piece and had to work incredibly hard—sometimes literally sweating—to earn a living wage.

209.

REPORT OF ACCIDENT.—*To Robert Baker, Esq., Inspector of Factories.*

Name, Age, and Occupation of Person injured .. *Martha Appleton aet 13 a Scavenger*

Name of Firm, situation of the Factory in which the Accident occurred, and nature of the work carried on .... *Messrs William Woods Son Cott & Sn Wallgate Wigan*

Date of Accident .... *Monday Aug 8th 1859*

Nature of Accident .... *Loss of all the fingers of the left hand*

Statement made to me by the injured person as to the cause of Accident, the hour of the day when it happened, and how that person was employed at the time .... *About 6.45 a.m. on Monday last I was at the back of the wheel house putting some bobbins in, when a giddiness came over me, and my hand slipped between the driving and main drum wheels of the self acting mules.*

TO TAILORS AND TAILORESSES !!!

GREAT
STRIKE
of
LONDON TAILORS
& SWEATER'S VICTIMS.

FELLOW WORKERS,

You are all aware that a Commission of Lords have been appointed to enquire into the evils of the Sweating System in the Tailoring Trade. The Revelations made before the Commission by Witnesses engaged in the Tailoring Trade, are a Disgrace to a Civilised Country. The Sweaters' Victims had hoped that this Commission, would have come to some satisfactory conclusion as to an alteration in the condition of the Sweated Tailors. Finding they have just put off their deliberation until Next Session, we have decided to take Immediate Action.

It is too long for us to wait, until Next Session, because the hardships inflicted upon us by the Sweater are unbearable. We have therefore decided to join in the CENERAL DEMAND FOR INCREASED COMFORT AND SHORTER HOURS OF LABOUR. Our Hours at present being on an average from 14 to 18 per day, in unhealthy and dirty dens.

WE DEMAND:

(1) THAT THE HOURS BE REDUCED TO 12 WITH AN INTERVAL OF ONE HOUR FOR DINNER AND HALF-HOUR FOR TEA.

(2) ALL MEALS TO BE HAD OFF THE PREMISES.

(3) GOVERNMENT CONTRACTORS TO PAY WAGES AT TRADE UNION RATES.

(4) GOVERNMENT CONTRACTORS AND SWEATERS NOT TO GIVE WORK HOME AT NIGHT AFTER WORKING HOURS.

We now Appeal for the support of all Tailors to join us and thus enable us to Successfully Enforce our Demands, which are reasonable.

Tailors & Tailoresses support in joining this General Strike.

We Appeal to all Tailors, Machinists, Pressers, Basters, &c. to meet EN-MASSE on THURSDAY, FRIDAY & SATURDAY MORNINGS, at 10 o'clock, (outside the Baths) GOULSTON STREET, WHITECHAPEL, E.

Piece Workers Finish Up, Week Workers Give Notice at Once,

ALL WORK TO CEASE ON SATURDAY AFTERNOON WHEN THE STRIKE WILL BE DECLARED.

Signed, STRIKE COMMITTEE.

Lewis Lyons, Chairman   Richard Rozelziy.   Annie Goodman.   Jacob Sydler,   M. Rosenthall.
J. Green   Phillip White.   L. Goldstein.   J. Margolin.   Harris Frank
J. Silverman   Simon Cohen   Charles Mowbray.   D. Greenbaum.   Lewis Portburg.
    W. Wess, Secretary.

Tailors Strike Committee Room "White Hart," Greenfield st., Commercial-Rd. All communications to be addressed to the Secty.

P.S. We appeal to those engaged in the Trade to at once join either of the following Societies:

AUGUST 20th, 1889

Introduction

Writing in the 1870s, a French worker, Norbert Truquin, wrote a detailed description of his youth. As a young boy, Truquin worked in wool combing, the process of straightening wool fibers before they were spun into yarn.

The comber takes a handful of wet wool in his right hand, and puts some oil, taken from a pot, on a finger of his left hand. He spreads this oil over the wool and greases the nearly red-hot comb. [Then] he takes a second comb . . . and combs the wool until the fibers have become straight and silky. . . . Next, the worker takes the tapered end of the wool out of his comb and draws it out a centimeter at a time until it is three or four feet long. He then passes the drawn wool to his young assistant who . . . removes . . . impurities with his teeth. [They] run like a string of rosary beads out of the two sides of his mouth. They use their teeth to extract the impurities because the wool has to be held taught so as not to risk tearing the strands apart, and their two hands cannot be spared from this task.

As distasteful (literally!) as Truquin's picture may seem, it described a scene that was not unusual before the industrial revolution. The work was skilled and very precise, it utilized very basic tools, and it involved an intimate relationship to the raw material and to the finished product. What came to be known as the industrial revolution utterly transformed work like this. It changed the techniques of production and manufacture, the organization and location of work, and workers' roles within industry. Beginning first in England in the late 1700s, industrialization would spread to other parts of Europe, to Russia, Japan, and beyond. Even parts of the globe that did not experience these changes directly experienced their consequences through trade, conquest, and colonial rule. Although historians now believe that this "revolution" actually occurred more slowly than was formerly thought, all agree that the changes that industrial capitalism brought to the European and North American landscapes were radical and far-reaching.

English men labor in front of a blazing furnace forging iron for the ships and bridges visible in the background. This dramatic portrayal of industrial progress attempted to convey all the advantages that iron and coal could bring.

Industrial Capitalism

The industrial revolution that began in eighteenth-century Britain was a capitalist revolution. It involved the accumulation of property and wealth—"capital"—that could be used for investment in industry and building factories, which is one of the hallmarks of industrialization. The profits made from producing goods under the system of factory production and the manufacture of new products increased the wealth of capitalists—middle-class investors in industry—and ultimately their power.

First and foremost, industrialization involved the application of new inventions and technologies to production. New machines harnessed sources of energy like water and steam power and made the manufacture of goods more efficient than ever. The large and complex machines that allowed industrial development could not, of course, fit in the small cottages in which artisans and laborers had toiled for generations. Industrialists thus built factories to house them in order to produce goods in large quantities for mass markets. The industrial centers, towns, and cities that sprang up around them were linked by an increasingly efficient system of roads, rivers and canals, and railways.

All of these changes deeply affected the lives and fortunes of workingmen and women. Large numbers of workers left small-scale, family-based production for jobs in mills and factories or to work as laborers digging canals, laying railways, or carting goods from ports and factories to markets and consumers. New machines and technologies also brought different ways of organizing work and new divisions of labor. Work that had formerly been accomplished by an individual artisan or skilled worker, working with his family, was now more sharply divided between several workers, each engaged in a different process or stage in production.

Nowadays, child labor is viewed as unusual, and in western Europe and North America it is illegal to employ school-age children, even though children continue to toil elsewhere—making rugs in Iran or carting bricks in India. Yet two centuries ago, child labor was less the exception than the norm. Children had always worked in agriculture and, like Norbert Truquin, in craft production. Once the industrial revolution occurred, they found jobs in factories. Women also routinely worked in agriculture, in home-based production, and as servants, as they had for centuries. With the industrial revolution they now worked in factories and their work became much more visible and prominent than ever before.

Great Britain was the first country to industrialize. Long before newly mechanized forms of production or factories appeared in America or France or even Germany, British entrepreneurs had begun to revolutionize cloth production and mining coal and iron, and British engineers were busy digging canals, planning networks of railroads, and building the first real factories—then called manufactories. The reasons that the British took the lead are simple. Britain had abundant natural resources that could be harnessed to provide energy for industrial manufacture: plentiful coal and iron reserves, as well as rivers that had long served as a means of transport. As a naval and imperial power since the 1600s,

Britain also benefited from the profits of trade, including the trade in slaves, and had developed a strong and efficient system of banking, credit, and insurance. These commercial institutions made it relatively easy to do business. Ideas about the importance of the individual's right to private property and a growing belief in the value of a free market also gained hold in Britain from the seventeenth century on, especially among the members of the middle class.

Eventually this new middle class of entrepreneurs would be able to promote its policies through Britain's parliamentary system. Finally, Britain had an additional critical resource: a free but largely landless labor force that needed to work for wages.

Gradually, other countries joined Britain in this industrial revolution. At the end of the eighteenth century and the beginning of the nineteenth century, most of America remained a country of small farms and plantations. A few cities dotted the eastern seaboard: Boston, New York, and Philadelphia. In America, just as in Britain, democratic ideology and belief in the freedom of producers flourished. After the American colonies freed themselves from the grip of British control in the American Revolution, the first textile factories appeared in the 1810s and 1820s along the banks of the Merrimack River in New England, employing young women and girls—the daughters of farmers in the surrounding countryside. Gradually factory industry spread south, to New Jersey and Pennsylvania.

France presented yet another pattern. After the French Revolution overthrew the monarchy in 1789, French businessmen, like their American counterparts, were freer to develop industry. But not until about the 1840s did industrialization pick up speed. French peasants remained strongly attached to their small farms and were unwilling to work in factories, and artisans and craft workers held tightly to their traditional forms of production. Even after industrial capitalism began to develop more fully, France remained a patchwork of factories, small farms, and workshops, until well into the twentieth century.

Not until the 1850s did Germany's industrial revolution begin in earnest. Blessed with excellent resources of iron and coal, Germany underwent rapid industrialization in the late nineteenth century. Mining, iron, and metalworking industries all flourished, as railroad building forced and fed off of the development of these heavy industries. Here, as in Britain, the state encouraged expanding industries, particularly after 1870 when Germany became a unified nation.

A Boston cleaning company boasts of its carpet-beating machine in an 1861 advertisement. The company claims the machine, a product of the industrial revolution in the United States, could clean carpets much more efficiently and effectively than a person could at home.

Smoke streams from a file and steel foundry in mid-nineteenth-century Sheffield, England. The busy factory and the carriages loaded with goods show how the industrial revolution looked from outside the factory.

Finally, after the 1870s, industrial revolutions occurred outside of western Europe and North America. Russia industrialized in the 1880s and 1890s, helped by rich reserves of iron and coal, government financial support, and an influx of capital from foreign investors. Japan also experienced an industrial revolution at roughly the same time and likewise benefited from government support of the textile industry and railways, which in turn stimulated the development of Japan's small iron and coal resources.

Wherever it occurred, the industrial revolution had dramatic effects on the people it touched. The great paradox of industrialization was that it brought both tremendous new wealth *and* terrible concentrations of poverty. While middle-class entrepreneurs profited enormously and became wealthy, working-class people experienced twelve- to fourteen-hour working days, increasingly rigorous work discipline, unsafe working conditions, industrial accidents, and often very low wages as well. Whereas middle-class businessmen could afford to live in spacious homes in green, leafy suburbs, far from the dirt and pollution of industrial districts, working-class men and women lived where they could afford to, in the shadow of the factory and workshop.

Although historians still debate the effects of industrialization on working peoples' standard of living, most agree that the vast economic wealth that the industrial revolution produced did not benefit everyone. Skilled male workers often found themselves in a privileged position within the labor force, able to command high wages, and to enjoy relative security of employment—at least as long as their skills were not displaced by machines. Less skilled men, whether they labored in new factories or old-fashioned workshops or at jobs building new cities, digging canals or laying railways or transporting goods and people, fared poorly. Women and children, most of whom were unskilled, took advantage of the new opportunities available in factories, but often reaped meager rewards for their intense efforts. The industrial revolution brought with it serious inequalities between the sexes. Employers routinely relegated women to unskilled jobs and reserved skilled jobs for men. Because factory owners believed that men should "bring home the bacon," they often paid men twice as much money as they paid women.

Workers deeply resented these inequalities, and they reacted—sometimes violently—to the enormous disparities in wealth and living standards that they saw around them and to the dreadfully low wages and dangerous conditions under which they worked. As industrial revolutions proceeded, workers became more organized in their opposition to these conditions. All over the globe, they formed labor unions and conducted strikes and protests to force employers to deal with them fairly. Workers also increasingly lent their support to labor or socialist parties, political parties that sought to represent the interests of working people and create a more equitable society. In these ways workers showed that they were not defenseless against the inexorable march of industrial change.

Making Sense of the Documents

Historians use a variety of documentary sources to study the industrial revolution. Visual materials—engravings, etchings, and paintings from the eighteenth and nineteenth centuries—that depict the new inventions spawned by industrialization allow us to see life inside the factory before the age of photography. From the mid-1800s on, photographs give us another view of workers' experience of industry. Although a picture may be worth a thousand words, historians are careful not to take the image as a totally faithful picture of reality. Many engravings from the early industrial era portray the factory as a smoothly working machine, but it is highly unlikely that factories were really that orderly or that clean. Historians "read" photographs critically, noticing how the subjects were posed and what the photographer chose to focus on. The choices of the photographer, painter, or engraver can themselves be of interest to the historian.

The same caution needs to be exercised in dealing with written accounts of factory life. Human beings produced the written documents that historians rely on for information about the past. Their class position, gender, race, and politics shaped their ideas. In an age where literacy rates of working-class people were notoriously low, many sources come from the middle class—factory owners, parliamentary representatives or government officials, and social reformers. Some of these observers proved to be especially critical of workers. They condemned what they saw as workers' irresponsibility and lack of thrift; others sought to promote the virtues of industrialization; still others criticized women's work, without taking into account that women, too, had to support their families. And some sympathized with the plight of laborers as they struggled to eke out an existence on meager wages. But even sympathetic social reformers often attempted to speak for the worker, often unconsciously imposing their own prejudices on the very people whom they attempted to help. When reading documents, historians continuously ask how the social position, gender, and race of the observer and the context of the document shape what is being said. They wonder if views of a middle-class observer writing about working-class life will accurately reflect the experience of workers. And they question whether anyone really has the right to represent the views of others. The claim of a social observer or reformer to "know" about the experience of a worker (or, in early nineteenth-century America, a slave) could be complicated by the observer's or reformer's political views, class, or race.

Fortunately, in spite of low literacy rates, workers did have a voice. They expressed themselves in a variety of ways and have left behind many valuable documentary sources that describe their lives in these rapidly changing times. British Parliamentary inquiries into the conditions and hours of work in the British textile industry in the 1830s provided an opportunity for workers to be heard. Testimony given by women and children, as well as men, spoke eloquently of the horrific conditions they faced in factory labor. There is no way to know how accurate their descriptions were. Some readers of these reports might be inclined to think that they were giving the Parliamentary commissioners a good line, or beefing up their stories in order to get Parliament to reduce their working hours and increase their wages. Giving

Angry Russian railway workers confront a manager with their demands for better working conditions and higher pay while police keep order in this painting of a 1905 train strike. The new machines and enormous economic progress that the industrial revolution created often came at the workers' expense, forcing them to toil in poor conditions at low wages.

testimony before a Parliamentary commissioner was, after all, not exactly a neutral situation. But again and again, workers all over the textile towns and cities cited the same problems.

Workers also left testimony of their views of the industrial revolution in the pamphlets and lists of demands that they drew up during the course of labor protests. Their words tell us a great deal about industrial conditions. Workers' poetry and songs can also be extremely informative. While poems and songs may express wistful yearnings or romanticize events, they also reveal something about the realities of workers' everyday lives or the hardships against which they reacted with music and rhyme. Finally, workers' autobiographies—like Norbert Truquin's—also offer insight into the experience of life in pre-industrial or industrial societies. Truquin's description of his work as a wool comber might have contained more than an ounce of exaggeration. Truquin wrote his account as an adult, some thirty years after the fact, and may have deliberately exaggerated the hardships he experienced as a youth. Checking other sources, however, historians have found Truquin's account to be reasonably accurate. This is the challenge of history: that what we know of the past was both lived and written. The truth probably lies somewhere in between.

Chapter One

Before the Industrial Revolution

Prior to about 1750, towns all across Europe and America bustled with activity. Artisans plied their trades in small workshops, merchants hawked their wares in the streets, and markets provided both festivity and opportunities for trade. In urban settings, skilled workers or artisans, primarily, but not exclusively men, worked at a variety of trades—from shoemaking to producing carpets and other fine textiles to furniture making—and typically produced goods of very high quality. In Europe, the birthplace of the industrial revolution, trades were highly regulated with details and standards set down by merchants and master craftsmen who exercised their control in organizations known as guilds.

The goods that craftsmen produced were often intended for export abroad or for consumption by wealthy urban merchants or aristocrats, hence the need for quality control. The guild system preserved and passed on skills and technical knowledge, but it was also conservative, discouraging innovation and limiting entry to the trade. The result was that, ironically, innovation, new methods, and products arose in the countryside, outside of towns and the watchful eyes of guilds. To understand the origins of modern industry, then, we must look first at rural society and agriculture. On the eve of the industrial revolution, a majority of Europeans—as well as Americans—lived in rural areas. What was life like for farmers and peasants who tilled the soil?

Traveling through France between 1787 and 1789, an English minister, Arthur Young, remarked in his diary on the small farms that dotted the countryside. "There cannot be a more pleasing spectacle . . ." he wrote, "than that of a family living on a little property, which their

The workers in this small family-run shop manufacture shoes by hand, as many craftsmen and women did before the industrial revolution. There are no sophisticated machines, and the finished products—boots, shoes, and slippers—hang from the rafters.

Guild Control

European guilds, associations of skilled producers—masters and apprentices—controlled access to different trades; they defined the skills that were necessary for production and ran the system of apprenticeship and training in those skills. They also maintained standards of how things were made and set the selling prices of goods. Some were lucky enough to obtain charters from the cities in which they operated—like the London Hatter's Guild in the seventeenth century—which gave them a virtual monopoly over the trade.

industry cultivates and perhaps created." Young was astonished at how French peasants managed to survive on small plots of land, eking out an existence by the sweat of their brows. In fact, in cottages and farmhouses almost everywhere, farmers and their families busily wove cloth and made straw hats or baskets, to provide extra income alongside farming. Britain, Europe, and America before about 1750 were all mainly rural societies, where families, sometimes with the aid of paid laborers or slaves (as in the American South), lived in the countryside and tilled the soil. Most farms were relatively small; farmers relied on rudimentary equipment and time-honored practices. Most worked with wooden plows and depended on horses or cattle to pull them; women spun thread on wooden spinning wheels or used long, grooved rods called distaffs; weavers wove fabric on wooden looms small enough to fit into the room of a house.

Whether in town or countryside, women and men tended to be relatively equal economic partners. Even when men and women did different work, the division of labor was often flexible. In Europe, as in America before the American Revolution, both men and women planted, cultivated, and harvested, while children and young people helped. Young people also milked cows, churned butter, gathered eggs, and fed farm animals. Similar activities occupied both men and women in early-nineteenth-century rural families in other parts of the world as far apart as Sweden, Japan, and some parts of Eastern Europe. Many families produced surpluses of agricultural produce, small animals and poultry, cheese, butter, and eggs to sell locally in market towns. In many communities, neighbors shared, bartered, and donated their labor to help each other out.

But not all laborers were free to till the soil or even to pick up and move from job to job as they chose. Slavery—the product of European traders' enslavement of Africans and Slavs—existed alongside other forms of bondage such as indenture and serfdom. Indentured servants agreed to work for a fixed term to pay off debts. Serfs labored on the estates of wealthy landlords in Russia and Eastern Europe. They received payment for their work, but were not free to come and go as they pleased. In North America and the Caribbean, African and African-American slaves labored on plantations, working in cotton, tobacco, and sugar cane fields. Getting slaves to the New World was a business in itself and a lucrative slave trade from Africa to the Caribbean and North America was part of the "Atlantic economy" that included commerce in

An Irish family prepares flax for spinning in their home in the 1780s. A mother and her daughters cut and comb out the fibers, while the father pulls fibers through iron prongs to reduce them to even smaller fibers, which will be spun into thread for weaving linen cloth.

cotton, tobacco, sugar, rum, and tea. The trade in human cargo permitted many British, French, and Spanish merchants to make huge profits. Some of these profits were later invested in industry, and slave-produced cotton became essential for the industrial revolution in late-eighteenth-century Britain.

Behind the scenes of traditional agricultural work, important changes were beginning that would profoundly alter the lives of men and women all over the world. An early form of industrial activity, typically referred to as "cottage industry" or the "putting out system," characterized the period from 1350 to 1750. Rural household members manufactured goods at home with simple tools, selling their products to merchants. Some historians see this system as a prelude to large-scale industrialization and refer to this early industrial activity as "proto-industrial." During this period, entrepreneurs accumulated the capital that would allow them to eventually build factories in Britain, the New World, and elsewhere. This form of rural manufacturing functioned in surprisingly similar ways in both Europe and America, where women and children labored alongside other family members at home, and agriculture and industry intersected.

In eighteenth-century America and Ireland, for example, women grew a plant called flax that they later spun into linen thread and wove into cloth. Rural women in France and England, who raised sheep and gathered and processed wool, spun it and wove it themselves or gave it to their fathers and husbands to weave. The merchants to whom rural producers sold their finished goods could make quite a profit from men and women working in their homes. Paying only for what the worker produced allowed businessmen to accumulate capital—the money that later could be invested in factories. This home-based production in rural areas grew up alongside traditional craft production located in towns and cities and provided a low-cost alternative to producing for a larger market. Urban guilds found it difficult to extend their control to rural areas and they grudgingly tolerated the coexistence of cottage production in the countryside.

At this time, major improvements in agriculture (sometimes called the agricultural revolution) began to allow farmers to feed growing numbers of people. In England, enterprising landlords, sanctioned by Parliament, enclosed common land previously used by poor peasants to pasture their animals. This practice forced thousands of poor rural dwellers to find jobs as agricultural laborers or as workers in cities. They provided a source of labor crucial to large-scale farming and to industry. Finally, improvements in transportation and commerce, and banking and finance, allowed goods to be traded more easily and allowed capital to circulate more freely. This period proved to be critical in preparing the ground for industrialization. The accumulation of money, or capital, to invest in industry, the gradual abolition of restrictions on production and commerce, the beginnings of improvements in transportation, and agricultural change all proved to be essential for the industrial revolution to occur.

Hard Work in the Countryside

In the centuries before the industrial revolution, rural society included a complex interweaving of farming and small-scale manufacturing. Martha Ballard, an eighteenth-century Maine midwife combined medicine, farming, and cloth production, as these entries from her diary from a few days in August 1787 illustrate. Women who struggle with balancing home and work in the contemporary world would have found Ballard's balancing act challenging, indeed.

flax

Plant grown commonly in North America and Europe. Its fibers were harvested, spun into thread, and woven to make linen cloth.

[August] 3 [, 1787] Clear & very hot. I have been pulling flax [the plant from which linen is made]. Mr. Ballard Been to Savages about some hay.

[August] 4 [, 1787] Clear morn. I pulld flax till noon. A very severe shower of hail with thunder and Litning began at half after one continued near 1 hour. I hear it broke 130 pains of glass in fort western. Colonel Howard made me a present of 1 gallon white Rhum & 2 lb sugar on account of my atendance of his family in sickness. Peter Kenny has wounded his leg & Bled Excesivily.

[August] 5 [, 1787] Clear morn. Mr Hamlin Breakfasted here. Had some pills. I was calld at 7 O clok to Mrs Howards to see James he being very sick with the canker Rash. Tarried all night.

[August] 7 [, 1787] Clear. I was Calld to Mrs Howards his morning for to see her son. Find him very low. Went from Mrs Howards to see Mrs Williams. Find her very unwell. Hannah Cool is there. From thence to Joseph Fosters to see her sick Children. Find Saray & Daniel very ill. Came home went to the field & got some very Cold water root. Then Calld to Mr Kenydays to see Polly. Very ill with the Canker. Gave her some of the root. I gargled her throat which gave her great Ease. Returned home after dark. Mr Ballard been to Cabesy. His throat is very soar. He gargled it with my tincture. Find relief & went to bed comfortably.

[August] 15 [, 1787] Clear morn. I pulld flax the fornon. Rain afternoon. I am very much fatagud. Lay on the bed & rested. The two Hannahs washing. Dolly weaving. I was called to Mrs Claton in travail [childbirth] at 11 O Clok Evening.

18   7 I spun some shoe thread & went to see Mrs Williams. Shee has news her Mother is very sick. Geny Huston had a Child Born the night before last. I was Calld to James Hinkly to see his wife at 11 & 30 Evening. Went as far as Mr Weston by land, from thence by water. Find Mrs Hinkly very unwell.

Although methods of production could be primitive, the at-home production of goods, such as cloth, involved a complex

This page of a diary kept by Martha Ballard, a Maine midwife, records her activities for the month of April 1789. She always began her diary by noting the weather, probably because she spent so much time outdoors, and then summarized the events of her day, which could include going to a neighbor's home to deliver a baby or traveling to a distant town to care for a sick person.

organization linking producers and consumers, with merchants playing a key role connecting them. In Aachen, Germany, the local woolen industry flourished thanks to the "putting out system." This report on rural textile manufacture, written in 1781 by a textile manager, Mr. Wintgens, describes how it all worked. Wintgen's report shows how each worker had a specialized task.

in the local manufactories . . . there are five main types of persons involved . . . the manufacturer, the weaver or draper, . . . the dyer, the fuller [a worker who cleaned, shrunk, and thickened cloth] and the finisher or shearer [who cut the nap off the cloth with large shears]. Each of these plays a leading part or has his own independent business . . . in completing . . . the work . . . so that the manufacturer need only supply the Spanish or Portuguese wool, which is exclusively used there.

the [merchant] . . . supplies [the weaver] with the necessary wool, weighed out in proportion to the number of pieces required. These weavers then have to get the wool washed, cleaned, . . . carded, spun, woven, and the nap raised, in other words, manufactured according to the fineness, the length, and breadth ordered, and delivered to the house of the manufacturer, so that the weavers of Aachen, taking into account the work performed within their stage, may be held to be [merchants] themselves . . . done . . . by others engaged for the purpose, some of whom live scattered in the villages and countryside.

When the pieces have been inspected and passed, they are sent to the fuller who sends them back to the entrepreneur's house after fulling. Now the finishers have their turn. . . . These finishers, after the cloths received by them have been cleaned, drawn, teased [the nap raised] and cropped twice, three or four times according to the quality . . . and once more and thus prepared for dyeing, hand them over direct to the dyers. . . . After dyeing, the cloths are returned to the finishers . . . and they provide the finishing touches, and . . . they are delivered back to the [merchant] for dispatch. Thus, in Aachen, the citizen . . . if he has enough resources to buy wool, and knows how to sell the cloths favourably, can become a . . . manufacturer, even if he has no other knowledge or skill of the cloth manufacture.

Peter Gaskell, a nineteenth-century English surgeon and observer of industrial change, described the pattern of home-based manufacture in England in his book *Artisans and*

A woman spins thread on a traditional spinning wheel in her home. Many women contributed valuable income to their families through this kind of work, but spinning machines in factories ultimately displaced them.

Machinery. **Although this book was published in 1836, well after the industrial revolution began in England, Gaskell looked back nostalgically to the period before factories began to dominate the English landscape. Gaskell suggests that workers had more independence and control as masters of their own trades when working in their own homes than in factories. His view of home-based manufacture was a bit idealistic, especially his view of its moral benefits. Gaskell believed that hard work built character and made men manly.**

Before the year 1760 . . . the majority of artisans had laboured in their own houses, and in the bosoms of their families. It may be termed the period of Domestic Manufacture; and the various mechanical contrivances were expressly framed for that purpose. The distaff, the spinning wheel, producing a single thread, and subsequently the jenny and mule, were to be found forming a part of the complement of household furniture in the majority of the cottage-homes of Great Britain, whilst every hamlet and village resounded with the clack of the hand-loom.

These were, undoubtedly, the golden times of manufactures, considered in reference to the character of the labourers. By all the processes being carried on under a man's own roof, he retained his individual respectability, he was kept apart from associations that might injure his moral worth, and he generally earned wages which were not only sufficient to live comfortably upon, but

jenny and mule

The spinning jenny allowed a spinner to produce eight threads simultaneously on eight spindles by tuning one wheel—an enormous increase in spinners' productivity. The spinning mule combined this feature of the jenny with an earlier invention, the water frame. The water frame (so named because it was powered by a water wheel) passed the thread through heavy iron rollers to make an even stronger twisted thread.

which enabled him to rent a few acres of land; thus joining in his own person two classes which are now daily becoming more and more distinct. It cannot, indeed, be denied, that his farming was too often slovenly, and conducted at times as a subordinate occupation; and that the land yielded but a small proportion of what, under a better system of culture, it was capable of producing. It nevertheless answered an excellent purpose. Its necessary tendence filled up the vacant hours, when he found it unnecessary to apply himself to his loom or spinning machine. It gave him employment of a healthy character, and raised him a step in the scale of society above the mere labourer. A garden was likewise an invariable adjunct to the cottage of the hand-loom weaver; and the floral tribes, fruits, and edible roots, were zealously and successfully cultivated.

The domestic manufacturers were scattered over the entire surface of the country. Themselves cultivators, and of simple habits and few wants, they rarely left their own homesteads. The yarn which they spun, and which was wanted by the weaver, was received or delivered, as the case might be, by agents, who traveled for the wholesale houses; or depots were established in particular neighbourhoods, to which they could apply at weekly periods. . . .

. . . the small farmer, spinner, or handloom weaver, presented an orderly and respectable appearance. He was a respectable member of society, a good father, a good husband, and a good son.

Gaskell's description, even if tainted with nostalgia for a mythical golden age, did describe in general terms the world of many eighteenth-century Europeans. Another view of domestic production appeared in a 1730 poem by an anonymous writer, who described an English household bustling with activity. One can almost hear the father of the family shouting orders to his wife, children, and helpers as they scurried about spinning, carding, combing, dying, and finishing cloth.

Quoth Maister—"Lads, work hard, I pray,
Clothmun [cloth must] be pearked [finished] next Market day.
And Tom mun go to-morn to t'spinners,
And Will mun seek about for t'swingers;
And Jack, to-morn, by time be rising,
And go to t'sizing house for sizing,
And get you web, in warping, done
That ye may get it into t'loom.

In the domestic economy of many Irish families in the early nineteenth century, the whole household participated in linen production. James Orr, an Irish weaver and poet, described this process in a poem entitled "The Penitent," written in 1804. Although the industrial revolution began in Britain around 1750, Orr's description suggests that families still carried out this form of production some sixty years later.

He weaved himself, and kept two or three
  going,
Who praised him for strong, well-handled
  yarn,
His thrifty wife and wise wee lasses span,
While warps and quills employed another
  child,
Some stripped each morn and threshed, the
  time to earn
To scamper with the hounds from hill to hill;
Some learned the question-book [schoolbook]
  in neighbouring barn—
Christy wrought very fine, at times drank a
  gill,
But when his web was out, had a hearty fill.

Men and women participate in flax scutching—the process of freeing the flax fibers from the woody portions of the plant—in the United States around 1860. Communities came together to beat flax so that the free fibers could be woven into linen cloth. Before industrialization, working collectively was more efficient than working alone and was also an occasion to socialize.

Joe—go give my horse some corn
For I design for [I'm going to] t'Wolds to-morn;
So mind and clean my boots and shoon,
For I'll be up it 'morn right soon!

"Mary—there's wool—tak thee and dye it
"It's that 'at ligs i th' clouted sheet!,
Mistress: "So thou's setting me my wark,
I think I'd more need mend thy sark [sock],
Prithie, who mun [sit] at' bobbin wheel?
And ne'er a cake at top o' the'creel!
And we to bake, and swing, to blend,
And milk, and barns [babes] to school to send,
And dumplins for the lads to mak,
And yeast to seek, and 'syk [such] as that'!
And washing up, morn, noon and neet,
And bowls to scald, and milk to fleet,
And barns to fetch again at neet!"

The Power of Guilds

Whereas rural dwellers freely combined domestic manufacture and agriculture, passing skills down from one generation to the next, in urban areas powerful guilds regulated

the training of workers and the quality and prices of goods. Within these typically male associations—women could only occasionally become guild members—master craftsmen employed a small number of apprentices in their workshops. The exclusion of women from these guilds made it extremely difficult for them to learn skilled trades, and is one reason they were relegated to unskilled and semiskilled jobs. These 1734 regulations from the guild of locksmiths, gun, watch- and spring makers in Germany illustrate how exacting some guilds could be in controlling the training of future masters. At the end of their training, apprentices had to make a "masterpiece" to demonstrate their competence in their trade.

III. A journeyman asking to be admitted to mastership of his craft, who has applied in due manner to the general assembly of the trade, shall make the following as his masterpiece:

A locksmith:

(1) A proper French or English lock.

(2) A table lock besides a padlock, with two keys in two levers, with rotating pinions, inside and out properly and well finished.

A lorimer shall make as his masterpiece:

(1) Two pairs of coach poles, similarly.

(2) Two pairs of riding poles similarly.

(3) A pair of stirrups, the bottoms and cross pieces welded in.

(4) A pair of spurs with hollow pricks.

A gun maker shall make as his masterpiece:

(1) A drawn musket, the barrel of five spans' length worked up in the most delicate manner, together with the stock and all the other parts.

(2) A pair of pistols after the present fashion, of iron, brass, and yellow metal or silver, so that each part is interchangeable with the other, no matter which of the two it is screwed into, with handle and accessories, all complete.

(3) A shotgun, the barrel of two ells length, with an ordinary lead, the lock to have a catch so that it cannot be fired without cocking, and does not work loose, together with the stock and accessories, all complete.

The barrels and the main components are to be forged by him according to the pattern shown to him in the gild, and within four weeks of the forging he must bring before the trade the barrels bored and filed as required, with screw threads and firing holes, when they will be tested by firing two bullets with full-strength powder.

lorimer

A maker of bits, stirrups, and spurs for riding horses

God blesseth trewe labour, / Be still quicke and kinde
With plentye and fauour, / Reward thou shalt finde

Pricke not at thy pleasure, / Be watchfull and wise
But in trewe honest measure / In goodnesse to alle : s

In heauen shall haue a place to dwell :

Four bakers illustrate the correct techniques for baking rolls in the guild ordinances of the Bakers of York, England, printed in the 1590s. The ordinances, or rules, state that bakers must "Pricke not at thy pleasure," but pay attention to the shape and size of the rolls and mark them in the correct place.

A clockmaker shall make as his masterpiece:

A standing clock which chimes at the quarter hour, shows the state of the moon and the days of the month, and goes for eight days before re-winding, with a drum-cylinder, and a long pendulum, to be used in a drawing room or bedroom. If he has been trained as a locksmith also and wishes to pursue that trade at the same time, he must make the masterpieces like other locksmiths. . . .

IV When the journeyman has been permitted to enter for the mastership by making his masterpiece, he shall forge it in the house of a master craftsman, and in his presence within 18 weeks. Clock and watchmakers who wish to enter for both, should be given more time. But it us by no means necessary for more than one master to be present: and all the feasting usually associated with these occasions is here prohibited.

V. When the masterpiece is finished, the candidate shall notify the master of the craft and the assessor, and ask them to inspect and judge his work. And this shall take place as soon as possible in the presence of the assessor.

If the completed masterpiece shall be found to have such faults as to show that the maker is not yet full master of his craft, he shall be ordered to improve the knowledge of his craft for a further period.

Guilds never gained a foothold in America. But even in Europe, guilds were doomed. In 1776, Anne Robert Jacques Turgot, finance minister under the French King Louis XVI, issued an edict banning guilds altogether. Turgot—like many manufacturers of his day—believed that the guilds, with their all their rules and regulations, stood in the way of economic progress. His edict illustrates how ideas about economic freedom began to develop in France. Although some guilds continued to operate in spite of Turgot's edict, they were finally outlawed once and for all during the French Revolution of 1789.

In nearly all the towns of our Kingdom the practice of different arts and crafts is concentrated in the hands of a small number of masters, united in a corporation, who alone have the exclusive right to manufacture and sell particular articles; so that those of our subjects who through wish or necessity intend to practice in these fields, must have attained the mastership, to which they are admitted only after very long tests, which are as difficult as they are useless, and after having satisfied rules or manifold exactions, which absorb part of the funds they need to set up in business or even to exist.

Those whose circumstances do not allow them to satisfy this expense, are reduced to having a precarious existence, under the domination of the masters, to languishing in poverty or taking

This ornate gilt bronze clock is one example of the luxury objects that skilled craftsmen in guilds produced in the eighteenth century. It took years to learn the techniques of shaping, molding, and gilding the bronze and enormous skill to execute them properly. These crafts and skills became increasingly rare as the industrial revolution advanced.

out of the country skills which might have been used to the State's advantage.

Citizens of all classes are deprived of their right of using workers whom they would like to employ and the advantages which competition confers in relation to the price and perfection of finished articles. One cannot execute the simplest tasks without having recourse to several workers from different corporations, without enduring their slowness, their dishonesty, and extortions. . . .

As far as the State is concerned, [guilds] ensure an incalculable reduction of commercial and industrial activity; the majority of our subjects suffer from a loss of wages and the means of subsistence; the inhabitants of the town in general are affected by subjection to exclusive privileges, similar in their effect to a . . . monopoly. . . . The spirit of monopoly that has prevailed [in the guild system] has been pushed so far as to exclude women from the tasks that are most suitable to their sex such as embroidery, which they cannot practice on their own account.

God, in giving man needs, by making work necessary, has made the right to work a universal prerogative, and this is the first, the most sacred, and the most indefeasible of all rights.

We regard it as one of the first duties of our law, and one of the acts most worthy of our charity, to free our subjects from all attacks against the inalienable right of mankind. Consequently, we wish to abolish these arbitrary institutions, which do not allow the poor man to earn his living; which reject a sex whose weakness has given it more needs and fewer resources, and which seem, in condemning it to an inevitable misery, to support seduction and debauchery; which destroy emulation and industry, and nullify the talents of those whose circumstances have excluded them from membership of a corporation; which deprive the State and the arts of all the knowledge brought to them by foreigners . . . ; which become an instrument of privilege and . . . raise above their natural level the price of those goods which are most essential for the people.

Anne Robert Jacques Turgot served as finance minister under King Louis XVI of France. He was extremely popular among the rising middle class in France, not only for abolishing guilds, and thereby paving the way for industrial innovation, but also for abolishing the tax exemptions long enjoyed by the French nobility.

Despite legislation banning guilds, they continued to function in France until the Revolution of 1789–1799 and didn't really disappear until legislation in 1792 (called the Le Chapelier law) outlawed all forms of worker and trade associations. On the eve of the Revolution, French women who attempted to support themselves in the home-based garment trades—commoners, known as the Third Estate—appealed to the king to protect their monopoly of sewing.

The women promised not to infringe on guild-regulated trades that were considered men's work, symbolized as "the compass or the square." Their petition illustrated the forces that Turgot's royal edict attempted to address thirteen years earlier.

The women of the Third Estate are almost all born without fortune; . . . Today . . . the difficulty of subsisting forces thousands of them . . . to throw themselves into cloisters where only a modest dowry is required, or . . . to hire themselves out when they do not have enough courage, enough heroism, to share the generous devotion of the daughters of Vincent de Paul. . . .

To prevent so many ills, Sire, we ask that men not be allowed, under any pretext, to exercise trades that are the prerogative of women—such as seamstress, embroiderer, seller of fashionable women's clothing etc., etc.; if we are left at least with the needle and spindle, we promise never to handle the compass or the square.

We ask, Sire, that your benevolence provide us with the means of putting to use the talents with which nature will have furnished us, notwithstanding the impediments which are forever being placed on our education.

May you assign us positions, which we alone will be able to fill, which we will occupy only after having passed a strict examination, after trustworthy inquiries concerning the purity of our morals.

We ask to be enlightened, to have work, not in order to usurp men's authority, but in order to be better esteemed by them, so that we might have the means of living out of the way of misfortune, and so that poverty does not force the weakest among us, who are blinded by luxury and swept along by example, to join the crowd of unfortunate beings who overpopulate the streets and whose debauched audacity is a disgrace to our sex.

Labor Bondage

Although the disappearance of guilds freed most white European workers from constraints on their mobility and training, not all workers labored freely. Africans and African Americans worked as slaves on the plantations of the American South. Indentured servants faced another form of labor bondage. Unlike a slave, one was not born into indenture, but agreed to work for low wages for a fixed period of time,

often to pay off a debt or in return for training or passage to the New World. This indenture contract was made by Thomas Smith, an English hatter, who bound out his young daughters, Esther and Ann, as servants to work in Samuel Greg's cotton mill in Lancaster, England, in 1788. The spelling of some of the words in this contract demonstrate the limits of education in eighteenth-century England.

Be it remembered, In this Day agreed by and between *Saml Greg of Manchester, in the County of Lancaster, Cotton Manufacturer* of the one Part, and *Thomas Smith, Hatters, of Heaton Norris in the country of Lancaster* of the other Part, as follows, That the said *Thos Smith Agreeath that Esther and Ann Smith* shall serve the said *Saml Greg* in his Cotton-Mills, in *Styall* as a just and honest servant, *Thirteen* Hours in each of the six working Days, and to be at *theair* own Liberty at all other Times; the Commencement of the Hours to be fixed from Time to Time by the said *Saml Greg* for the Term of *Three* Years at the Wages of *one Penney per Week and Sufficient Meat, Drink and Apparell Lodging washing and all other Things necessary and fit for a Servant.*

  And that if the said *Esr and Ann Smith* shall absent *themselves* from the Service of the said *Saml Greg* in the said working Hours, during the said Term, that the said *Saml Greg* may not only abate the

THREE POUNDS REWARD.

RUN AWAY from the Subscriber, living at Warwick furnace, Minehole, on the 23d ult. an Irish servant man, named DENNIS M'CALLIN, about five feet eight inches high, nineteen years of age, has a freckled face, light coloured curly hair. Had on when he went away, an old felt hat, white and yellow striped jacket, a new blue cloth coat, and buckskin breeches; also, he took with him a bundle of shirts and stockings, and a pocket pistol; likewise, a box containing gold rings, &c. Whoever takes up said servant and secures him in any goal, so as his master may get him again, shall have the above reward and reasonable charges paid by   JAMES TODD.

  N. B. All masters of vessels, and others, are forbid from harbouring or carrying him off, at their peril.

An advertisement from a 1772 Pennsylvania newspaper offers a reward for the return of a runaway indentured servant. Although indentured servants were obliged to serve a term of up to seven or eight years, many could not stand the harsh conditions of service and escaped before their term was up.

In this cartoon, landowners play cards using bundles of serfs as their stakes in the game. Russian serfs indeed suffered terrible mistreatment by the men who employed them on their estates, as this satirical cartoon implies. Landowners tended to see serfs as property and not as people.

Wages proportionably, but also for Damages sustained by such Absence. And that the said *Saml Greg* shall be at Liberty during the Term, to discharge the Servant from his Service, for Misbehavior, or want of Employ.

As Witness their Hands, this *Twenty Eight Day* of *Jany* 1788—

Witness   By me Thomas Smith
Mattw Fawkner

Another form of labor bondage, serfdom, existed in Eastern Europe and Russia. Unlike slavery, where workers were bought and sold and had no legal rights, and indentured servitude, where workers agreed to work for a fixed term for wages, serfs were not bought and sold and did have some legal rights. They were viewed as the property of landowners and were required to work on specific estates or farms for life. Although serfdom declined in most parts of western Europe prior to 1800, it remained legal in Russia until 1861. English traveler William Coxe described the conditions of Russian serfs in a diary that he kept during his travels to Russia in 1784.

Peasants belonging to individuals are the private property of the landholders, as much as implements of agriculture, or herds of cattle; and the value of an estate is estimated, as in Poland, by the number of [serfs] and not by the number of acres. No regulations have tended more to rivet the shackles of slavery in the empire than the two laws of Peter the Great, one which renders the landholder accountable to the crown for the poll-tax of his [serfs]; the other, which obliges him to furnish a certain number of recruits [to the czar]; for by these means he becomes extremely interested that none of his peasants migrate, without permission, from the place of their nativity. These circumstances occasion a striking difference in the fate of the Russian and Polish peasants, even in favor of the latter, who in other respects are more wretched. If the Polish boor [serf] escapes to another master, the latter is liable to no pecuniary penalty for harboring him; but in Russia, the person who receives another's [serf] is subject to a heavy fine. With respect to his own demands upon his peasants, the lord is restrained by no law, either in the exaction of any sum, or in the mode of employing them. He is absolute master of their time and labor; some he employs in agriculture; a few he makes his menial servants, and perhaps without wages; and from others he exacts an annual payment.

Rural Revolution

Around the 1700s, enormous changes occurred in agriculture and domestic manufacture. In England, in order to increase the size of their holdings and also to farm more efficiently, enterprising landlords threw up fences around common lands, which were not privately owned and therefore available for anyone to use. Parliament, controlled by some of these same landowners, sanctioned the process, known as enclosures. By 1815, large landowners had fenced off more than a million acres. Many landless peasants who were deprived of common land for pasturing animals or planting, now hired themselves out as day laborers on newly enlarged estates and farms. Others migrated to cities. In 1795, the Reverend David Davies wrote an essay in which he described this process and reflected on the miserable state of rural laborers.

The practice of enlarging . . . farms, and especially that of depriving the peasantry of all landed property, has contributed greatly to increase the number of dependent poor.

1. The land-owner, to render his income adequate to the increased expense of living, unites several small farms into one, raises the rent to the utmost, and avoids the expense of repairs. The rich farmer also [encloses] as many farms as he is able to stock; lives in more credit and comfort than he could otherwise do; and out of the profits of the *several farms*, makes an ample provision for

The French painter Jean-François Millet, touched by the hardships of rural life, painted countless images of peasants toiling in the countryside of nineteenth-century France. This painting, Man with a Hoe, depicts the hardscrabble existence of French peasants whose exhausting labor put food on the table.

one family. Thus thousands of families, which formerly gained an independent livelihood on those separate farms, have been gradually reduced to the class of day-labourers. But day-labourers are sometimes in want of work and are sometimes unable to work; and in either case their resort is [charity]. It is a fact, that thousands of parishes have not now half the number of farmers which they had formerly. And in proportion as the number of farming families has decreased, the number of poor families has increased.

2. The depriving the peasantry of all landed property has [made beggars of] multitudes. It is plainly agreeable to sound policy, that as many individuals as possible in a state should possess an interest in the soil, because this attaches them strongly to the country and its constitution, and makes them zealous and resolute in defending them. But the gentry of this kingdom seem to have lost sight of this wise and salutary policy. Instead of giving to the laboring people a valuable stake in the soil, the opposite measure has so long prevailed, that but few cottages, comparatively, have now *any* land about them. Formerly many of the lower sort of people occupied tenements of their own with parcels of land about them, or they rented such of others. On these they raised for themselves a considerable part of [what they lived on], without being obliged, as now, to buy all they want at shops. And this kept numbers from [relying on charity]. But since those small parcels of ground have been swallowed up in the contiguous farms and enclosures, and the cottages themselves have been pulled down; the families which used to occupy them are crowded together in decayed farm houses, with hardly enough ground about them for a cabbage garden: and being thus reduced to be *mere* hirelings, they are of course very liable to come to want. And not only the *men* occupying those tenements, but their *wives and children* too, could formerly, when they wanted work abroad, employ themselves profitably at home; whereas now, few of *these* are constantly employed, except in harvest; so that almost the whole burden of providing for their families rests upon the *men*. Add to this, that the former occupiers of small farms and tenements, though poor

themselves, gave away something in alms to their poorer neighbours; a resource which is now much diminished.

Thus an amazing number of people have been reduced from a comfortable state of partial independence to the precarious position of hirelings, who, when out of work, must immediately come to their parish. And the great plenty of working hands always to be had when wanted, having kept the price of labour down below its proper level, the consequence is universally felt in the increased number of dependent poor.

By the early nineteenth century, landlords in Germany took advantage of new knowledge of agriculture and husbandry that was beginning to circulate throughout Europe and practiced new methods such as crop rotation. Farmers produced more food and could feed more and more people living in urban areas. In 1823, Johann Elsner Gottfried, an authority on sheep farming, wrote a study about the improvements made by a farmer, Herr von Keltsch, on one of his estates in Silesia, in northwestern Germany.

In order to give you an idea of the larger estates in this region, I will take you into one of them, distinguished by the great industry and attention with which it is conducted. . . . Herr von Keltsch may rightly be considered an agriculturalist who has, in the course of many years experience in his own practice, developed a method which ensures that he almost always gets good results. . . .

First, we inspect his livestock. The cattle kept by him here are a genuine Swiss cross. . . . The strain is distinguished by strength, well-fed appearance and cleanliness. Comparing them with the miserable, starving and misshapen specimens one finds here and there, it hardly seems as though they were the same kind of animal.

Herr v. K's flocks of sheep have reached a fair degree of fineness in their wool, since he has done a great deal towards this in recent years, and they improve every year. The grasses and herbs of the fertile soil of this region have the power of improving not only the quality of the wool, but also its quantity. You may call this a paradox, but it is nevertheless true; for the beneficial effect of the grazing and fodder available here on the quality is confirmed by the high repute in which the fleeces of this region have been held for a long time among the wool buyers. . . .

I now turn to the arable system of cultivation of this region. The three-field system [of rotating crops between fields] is still in the main observed here. . . . [T]he so-called fallow [part of a three-field

As far as the eye can see, fields in the early eighteenth-century English countryside were divided by hedges. Some big landowners accumulated relatively extensive estates through the process of enclosures, which allowed landowners to fence off portions of common land for their own benefit.

system] has one part clover and one part peas and beans. Potatoes are frequently introduced into the summer field as a fourth crop but where this is not done, they are planted in the fallow and followed by the winter, and sometimes even the summer crop. After the pure fallow comes wheat, but also in many parts some clover, which is then ploughed in time and broken up before sowing; the rest is sown with rye. After the wheat follows flax, where there has been clover, and barley with clover where there was pure fallow. It is always so arranged that flax and Clover are alternatives, i.e. where there was flax the last time, clover is sown, and vice versa; where there have been peas and beans, there follow oats, to become fallow the next year.

Whereas some rich landowners in England practiced enclosures for raising sheep, others grew crops such as flax (used to make linen) and employed workers on their estates in small "manufactories" to spin the fibers into linen thread. The Reverend Arthur Young, who toured Ireland in the years 1776–1778, wrote about this development in his travel diary. Young described Mr. French, an energetic farmer near the town of Moniva, Ireland. Mr. French participaed in a process that came to be known as the agricultural revolution: he improved his land, rotated his crops between fields, used fertilizer, and took better care of his livestock. His activities show that the industrial revolution really began in the countryside. The spirit of enterprise had taken hold.

Dividing [his] lands into divisions of from fifteen to twenty-acred pieces, [he cleared] them of stones. . . . They are all lime-stone lands and make very fine sheep walks. Before the improvement, very many sheep died on these grounds. . . . but since the liming, this has not happened; nor would it before give flax, but now very fine.

Mr. French burns . . . lime in perpetual kilns with turf. . . . Another sort of mountain land, the wet boggy sort, one to four feet deep; which he improved by digging off almost all the bog for lime; then ploughed it with six bullocks and let it to the poor from a guinea to thirty shillings an acre, to . . . plant potatoes; after which they pay as much more for a crop of oats. Then limes it, takes another crop of oats, and sows grasses with it; after this improvement, lets as well as the other. In the year 1744, when Mr. French came to his estate, there was no other linen manufacture than a little . . . linen, merely for [farmers'] own consumption, with no other spinning than for that, and even with this, there was not more than one loom in 100 cabbins. In 1746, he undertook to establish a better fabric. . . . He first began by erecting spinning schools and sowing flax, twenty-one acres of which he sowed on his own account. The linen board [the Irish Linen Board regulated the production of linen] gave at that time one penny a day to any children that went to any spinning schools, which was of use, but the providing flax Mr. French found of the greatest use. In 1749, he established eight weavers and their families, and the same year, built a bleach mill, and . . . sent a lad into the north [the heart of Irish linen production], and bound him apprentice there, in order to learn the whole business. Upon his return, he managed the manufactory for Mr. French, buying the yarn, paying weavers for weaving it by the yard, bleaching and felling it. . . . The progress of this undertaking, united with the agricultural improvements, will be seen by the following returns of the Moniva estate, at different periods.

In 1744. There were three farmers and six or eight shepherds and cow-herds.

In 1771. There were two hundred and forty-eight houses, ninety looms, and two-hundred sixty-eight [spinning] wheels.

In 1772. Two hundred and fifty-seven houses, ninety-three looms, and two hundred eighty-eight wheels.

In 1776. Two hundred seventy-six houses, ninety-six looms, and seventy [spinning] wheels.

Chapter Two

The Age of Machines

In some ways the industrial revolution was a fortunate accident. A winning combination of crucial elements came together over the course of the eighteenth and nineteenth centuries to produce a sudden spurt of industrial activity, first in England and later elsewhere in America, Europe, and other parts of the world. This happened, in part, because of demand. As a result of dramatic population growth in the 1700s, the demand for cheap clothing rose. In England, for instance, manufacturers who profited from the "putting out system," by employing rural dwellers laboring in their homes, realized that their profits might be even greater if they could exert more control over their labor force and over the labor process. The agricultural revolution, by improving crop yields, made it possible to free large numbers of workers from the need to grow their own food. Enclosures had already produced hundreds of landless laborers available to take unskilled jobs in industry. Meanwhile, inventors and scientists developed new ways of improving and speeding up production.

One invention followed another, revolutionizing cloth production. In 1733, John Kay invented a flying shuttle, which enabled a weaver to propel the shuttle from one side of the loom to another with the force of his arm. This simple invention sped up weaving so considerably that for a while English weavers suffered from a shortage of thread. It took more than thirty years before James Hargreaves helped to solve this problem in 1764 with an invention known as the spinning jenny, which spun thread much more efficiently than the spinning wheel. But Richard Arkwright's water frame four years later made it possible to spin several strong, even threads simultaneously. This new technology revolutionized spinning and spurred developments in other areas. When James Watt invented an improved steam engine in 1776, the stage was set for a revolution in cloth production. Once steam was applied to run a mechanized loom, it could produce seven

Several men place a hot piece of iron into the massive steam hammer of a French iron forge around 1860. The noise must have been deafening and the heat was intense.

times the cloth that a hand loom could yield. Skilled hand-loom weavers would soon be out of business. The age of the machine had begun.

These new machines were expensive and much too large for the relatively small "manufactories," as the early factories were called, that dotted the English countryside. Large factories were the logical solution. Merchant manufacturers used the profits they accumulated in the rural textile business or in the Atlantic slave trade to build huge buildings to house the machines and the workers to run them. They drew on a ready labor supply in the hundreds of men, women, and children thrown off the land by enclosures or born in England's late-eighteenth-and-early-nineteenth-century population explosion. A new division of labor, separating men's work and women's work—what historians call the "gender division of labor"—was born inside the factory gates. Typically, women ran the spinning machines and the machines that wound the thread on wooden spindles known as bobbins. Men cleaned and adjusted the machines, ran the power looms, and supervised work. Believing that women worked only to supplement the wages of husbands and fathers, and that women's labor was worth less than men's, employers paid them less than men as well.

The machine and the factory symbolized the enormous changes brought about by sustained (and long-term) industrialization everywhere. Machines made irrelevant skills learned over years of work experience or in the process of guild apprenticeships, such as hand-loom weaving or shoemaking. Inside the fac-

Invented by English weaver and carpenter James Hargreave, the spinning jenny, which enabled a spinner to spin multiple threads at once, eventually put thousands of women home spinners out of work. Though it was small enough to be used in a workshop, it was too cumbersome to fit into the average worker's home.

tory, employers held workers to a fixed working day; supervisors and overseers made sure that workers remained at work except for the odd meal break until the evening factory bell rang. Factory hands had to keep up with the pace of the machine and the discipline of the clock, rather than work at their own pace.

But as prevalent as mechanization seemed, and as much as industrialization changed the face of Britain and eventually of other countries, other factors, namely ideas, also played an important role in economic change. Political economists—men who wrote about the relationship between the economy, society, and government—helped to create a climate in which industry would thrive. They provided the ideas that stimulated individual initiative and innovation and in turn drove industrial development. In addition, neither the machine nor the factory took over all at once. For one thing, not all workers were eager to take up factory employment. In some areas of Europe, they could earn more as agricultural workers and, at least up to the 1840s, only a minority of European workers worked in factories. Moreover, throughout the nineteenth century, industrialization occurred unevenly over the globe—so much so that some historians even prefer not to speak of an industrial revolution at all. In Ireland, for instance, small linen producers continued to weave linen cloth in rural cottages at the same time as factories spewed forth smoke and fumes across the Irish Sea. In France, although iron and cotton textile factories appeared in the mid-1800s, at the end of the nineteenth century, large numbers of women still sewed lingerie or made artificial flowers in their cramped Parisian apartments. Russia and Japan did not experience industrial revolutions until late in the nineteenth century. In spite of this, there is no question that everywhere they occurred, industrial revolutions permanently altered the ways that work was done and the lives of workers as well. The social and economic gap that separated the humble factory operative from the middle-class factory owner or the banker stood out in sharp relief as industry advanced.

The New Spirit of Enterprise

In 1776, Adam Smith, a Scottish philosopher, published a book destined to become a best-seller, *An Inquiry into the Nature and the Causes of the Wealth of Nations*. Smith attacked the system of economic regulation then prevalent in England and in much of the rest of Europe at the time. This system, known as mercantilism, involved state regulation of

Now cotton yarn is cheaper than linen yarn, and cotton goods are very much used in place of cambric, lawns, and other expensive fabrics of flax, and they have almost totally superseded the silks. Women of all ranks from the highest to the lowest, are clothed in British manufactures of cotton, from the muslin cap on the crown of the head to the cotton stockings under the sole of the foot. . . . With the gentlemen, cotton stuffs for waistcoats have almost superseded woolen cloths, and silk stuffs, I believe, entirely.

—David MacPherson, *Annals of Commerce*, 1805

economic activity, with the goal of increasing national wealth. In *The Wealth of Nations,* Smith argued that there was a better way to increase the "wealth of nations": governments should let individuals do as they wished in all spheres of the economy. The French term *laissez-faire,* meaning "let do," encapsulated Smith's idea that the "invisible hand" of the market was all that was needed to generate economic growth.

It is only for the sake of profit that any man employs a capital in the support of industry; and he will always, therefore, endeavour to employ it in the support of that industry of which the produce is likely to be of the greatest value, or to exchange for the greatest quantity either of money or of other goods. . . . As every individual, therefore, endeavours as much as he can both to employ his capital in the support of domestick industry, and so to direct that industry that its produce may be of the greatest value; every individual necessarily labours to render the annual revenue of the society as great as he can. He generally, indeed, neither intends to promote the publick interest, nor knows how much he is promoting it. . . . [H]e intends only his own security; and by directing that industry in such a manner as its produce may be of the greatest value, intends only his own gain, and he is in this, as in many other cases, led by an invisible hand to promote an end which was no part of his intention. Nor is it always the worse for the society that it was not part of it. By pursuing his own interest, he frequently promotes that of the society more effectually than when he really intends to promote it. . . .

Let the . . . natural liberty of exercising what species of industry they please be restored to all his majesty's subjects, in the same manner as to soldiers and seamen; that is, to break down the exclusive privileges of corporations, and repeal the statute of apprenticeship, both which are real encroachments upon natural liberty, and add to these the repeal of the law of settlements, so that a poor workman, when thrown out of employment either in one trade or in one place, may seek for it in another trade or in another place, without the fear either of a prosecution or of a removal, and neither the publick nor the individuals will suffer.

Samuel Smiles, an English writer, agreed with Smith's ideas about the importance of individual freedom for economic growth and prosperity. He celebrated what he believed to be English values—nationalism, empire, and English "racial"

Adam Smith, author of The Wealth of Nations, *believed that in a "well governed society," the division of labor would produce a "universal opulence which extends itself to the lower ranks of the people."*

superiority—that allegedly promoted industrial growth. In his 1859 book *Self Help, with Illustrations of Character and Conduct,* mainly addressed to middle-class men, Smiles argued that more than industriousness was needed for success: masculine respectability had to be cultivated as well. He quoted the words of Ambroise Rendu, an early nineteenth-century French authority on education.

National progress is the sum of individual industry, energy, and uprightness, as national decay is of individual idleness, selfishness, and vice. . . . the highest patriotism and philanthropy consist, not so much in altering laws and modifying institutions, as in helping and stimulating men to elevate and improve themselves by their own free and independent action as individuals. . . . English institutions . . . give free action to every man and woman and will recognize an educator in each, cultivate the citizen, ready alike for the business of practical life and the responsibilities of the home and the family. And although our schools and colleges may, like those of France and Germany, turn out occasionally forced specimens of over-cultured minds, what we may call the national system does on the whole turn out the largest number of men, who, to use Rendu's words, "reveal to the world those two virtues of a lordly race—perseverance in purpose, and a spirit of conduct which never fails."

It is this individual freedom and energy of action . . . recognized by . . . observant foreigners, that constitutes the prolific source of our national growth. For it is not to one rank or class alone that this spirit of free action is confined, but it pervades all ranks and classes: perhaps its most vigorous outgrowths being observable in the commonest orders of the people. . . .

One of the most strongly marked features of the English people is their indomitable spirit of industry, standing out prominent and distinct in all. . . . It is this spirit, displayed by the [common people] of England, which has laid the foundations and built up the industrial greatness of empire at home and in the colonies. This vigorous growth of the nation has been mainly the result of the free industrial energy of individuals. . . .

"Respectability" in its best sense is good—it means a person worth regarding, worth turning back to look at. But the respectability that consists merely in keeping up appearances is not worth looking at in any sense. Far better and more respectable is the good poor man than the bad rich one. . . . [A] well balanced and well stored mind, a life full of useful purpose, whatever the

> "Indeed some of the finest qualities of human nature are intimately related to the right use of money, such as generosity, honesty, justice, and self-sacrifice; as well as the practical virtues of economy and providence."
>
> —Samuel Smiles, *Self-Help with Illustrations of Character and Conduct*, 1859

position occupied in it may be—is of far greater importance than the average worldly respectability. The highest object of life we take to be to form a manly character and to work out the best development possible of body and spirit. . . . This is the end: all else ought to be regarded but as the means. Accordingly, that is not the most successful life in which a man gets the most pleasure, the most money, the most power or place, honor or fame; but that in which a man gets the most manhood and performs the greatest amount of useful work and of human duty.

The ideas of Adam Smith, Samuel Smiles, and Scottish scientific writer Andrew Ure encouraged the new middle class that emerged in nineteenth-century Europe. Freed from government restraints, some enterprising businessmen built small factories and gradually expanded their properties or bought other small factories nearby. In an 1839 letter to a business associate, William Grant, the son of a failed British cattle dealer, described his family's rise from humble beginnings, through an astute business sense and hard work, to success in the textile business. Although Grant's father was unable to obtain work at the mill of Richard Arkwright, the inventor of the spinning jenny, Grant learned about cloth printing and eventually entered the business himself. William Grant's story was not entirely atypical, although most young men did not rise so quickly into the ranks of successful middle-class entrepreneurs.

Springside, May 17, 1839.

Dear Sir,—Allow me to acknowledge the receipt of your esteemed favour of the 10th. My father was a dealer in cattle, and lost his property in the year 1783. He got a letter of introduction to Mr. Arkwright (the late Sir Richard) and came by way of Skipton and Manchester, accompanied by me. As we passed along the old road, we stopped for a short time on the Park estate to view the valley. My father exclaimed, "What a beautiful valley! May God Almighty bless it!" It reminded me of Speyside, but the Irwell is not so large as the river Spey. I recollected that Messrs. Peel & Yates were then laying the foundation of their printworks at Ramsbottom. We went forward to Manchester and called upon Mr. Arkwright, but he had so many applications then he could not employ him. There were then only Arkwright's mill, on a small scale, and Thacary's . . . mill in Manchester. There was a mill on the Irwell belonging to Mr. Douglas, two belonging to Messrs.

Peel & Yates, the one at Radcliffe Bridge the other at Hinds; and these were the only mills then in Lancashire. My father then applied to Mr. Dinwiddie, a Scotch gentleman, who knew him in his prosperity, and who was a printer and manufacturer at Hampson Mill, near Bury. He agreed to give my father employment, and placed my brother James and me in situations, where we had an opportunity of acquiring a knowledge both of manufacturing and printing; and offered me a partnership when had finished my apprenticeship. I declined his offer, and commenced business for myself on a small scale, assisted by my brothers John, Daniel, and Charles, and removed to Bury, where I was very successful, and in the course of a few years . . . I removed to Manchester, and [began] printing in partnership with my brothers. My brother Daniel [traveled] through the North of England and almost to every market town in Scotland. In 1806 we purchased the print works belonging to Sir Robert Peel, & etc., situated at Ramsbottom. In 1812, we purchased Nuttall factory. In consequence of the death of Mr. Alsop, the workpeople had been long short of employment and were very destitute. We ordered the manager to get new machinery of the first rate construction, and greatly extended the building; and before we began to spin or manufacture we clothed the whole of the hands at our own expense, prepared an entertainment for them, and observed that the interests of masters and servants are bound together, that there are reciprocal duties to perform, that no general or admiral could be brave unless he was supported by his men, that we knew how to reward merit, and would give constant employment and liberal wages to all faithful servants and I am happy to say that they, as well as those at our printing establishments, with very few exceptions, have Conducted themselves with great propriety.

In 1818 we purchased Springside, and in 1827 we purchased the Park estate, and erected a monument to commemorate my father's first visit to this valley, and on the very spot where he and I stood admiring the scenery below. There is a very fine view from the top of the tower on a clear day, and the Welsh hills can be described in the distance.

A heavy cast-iron cylinder used in early steam engines leaves the Coalbrookdale ironworks on a wagon pulled by a team of horses. The iron foundry, to the right of the cylinder, was typical of factories that sprang up in the English countryside.

We attribute much of our prosperity, under divine Providence, to the good example and good counsel of our Worthy parents. . . . We have done business on a large scale . . . exporting our goods and receiving the productions of those countries in return.

The Force of Steam

New machines and inventions were the hallmark of the industrial revolution. James Watt's steam engine, patented in England in 1769, powered locomotives on the first railroads in England and the United States. Steam also powered looms and other industrial machines. Artists and writers marveled at (and also deplored) how industry transformed the English landscape. Indeed, the "industrial novel" became a literary form in its own right. In 1843, novelist Charles Dickens described a factory town and its workers in his novel _Hard Times_.

The Fairy palaces burst into illumination, before pale morning showed the monstrous serpents of smoke trailing themselves over Coketown. A clattering of clogs upon the pavement; a rapid ringing of bells; and all the melancholy mad elephants, polished and oiled up for the day's monotony, were at their heavy exercise again.

Stephen bent over his loom, quiet, watchful, and steady. A special contrast, as every man was in the forest of looms where Stephen worked, to the crashing, smashing, tearing piece of mechanism at which he laboured. Never fear, good people of an anxious turn of mind, that Art will consign nature to oblivion. Set anywhere, side by side, the work of GOD and the work of man; and the former, even though it be a troop of Hands of very small account, will gain in dignity from the comparison.

So many hundred Hands in this Mill; so many hundred horse Steam Power. It is known, to the force of a single pound weight, what the engine will do; but not all the calculators of the National Debt can tell me the capacity for good or evil, for love or hatred, for patriotism or discontent, for the decomposition of virtue into vice, or the reverse, at any single moment in the soul of one of these its quiet servants, with the composed faces and the regulated actions. There is no mystery in it; there is an unfathomable mystery in the meanest of them, for ever. Supposing we were to reserve our arithmetic for material objects, and to govern these awful unknown quantities by other means!

Alongside steam, new ways of organizing labor also accelerated production. Scottish political economist Adam Smith believed that dividing the manufacture of goods into their component parts would lead to greater efficiency. This is what he observed in his book The Wealth of Nations _in 1776 about the business of making pins._

In the way in which this business is now carried on, not only the whole work is a particular trade, but it is divided into a number of branches, of which the greater part are likewise particular trades. One man draws out the wire, another straightens it, a third cuts it, a fourth points it, a fifth grinds it at the top for receiving the head; to make the head requires two or three distinct operations, to put it on, is a peculiar business, to whiten the pins is another; it is even a trade by itself to put them into the paper; and the important business of making a pin is, in this manner, divided into about eighteen distinct operations, which, in some manufactories, are all performed by distinct hands, though in others, the same man will sometimes perform two or three of them. I have seen a small manufactory of this kind where ten men only were employed, and where some of them consequently performed two or three distinct operations. Those ten persons . . . [made] among them upwards of forty-eight thousand pins in a day.

An English miner stands in front of a steam engine pulling coal wagons, which were first used to transport coal in the early nineteenth century. He carries a lunch basket because workers had to take their meals in the mines, emerging into daylight only at the end of their workday.

The day grew strong, and showed itself outside, even against the flaming lights within. The lights were turned out, and the work went on. The rain fell, and the Smoke-serpents, submissive to the curse of all that tribe, trailed themselves upon the earth. In the waste-yard outside, the steam from the escape pipe, the litter of barrels and old iron, the shining heaps of coals, the ashes everywhere, were shrouded in a veil of mist and rain.

The work went on, until the noon-bell rang. More clattering upon the pavements. The looms, and wheels, and Hands all out of gear for an hour.

In his 1835 book, *The Philosophy of Manufactures*, English economist Andrew Ure argued that ultimately machines would replace handworkers, and unskilled women and children would replace skilled men.

It is in fact, the constant aim and tendency of every improvement in machinery to supersede human labor altogether, or to diminish its cost, by substituting the labor of women and children for that of men; or that of ordinary laborers for trained artisans. . . . The proprietor of a factory in Stockport states . . . that by such substitution, he would save fifty pounds a week in wages, in consequence of dispensing with nearly forty male spinners, at about twenty-five shillings of wages each. . . .

Had British industry not been aided by Watt's invention it must have gone on with a retarding pace . . . and would . . . have experienced an insurmountable barrier to further advancement. . . .

Englishman James Watt invented a version of the steam engine that powered machines faster and more continuously than any equipment powered by humans. Watt's engine was applied to everything from spinning machines to looms, train engines, and even machines for extracting coal.

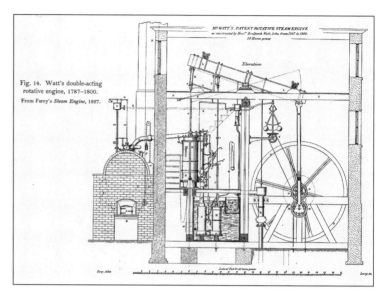

Fig. 14. Watt's double-acting rotative engine, 1787–1800. From Farey's *Steam Engine*, 1827.

Steam engines furnish the means not only of their support but of their multiplication. They create a vast demand for fuel; and, while they lend their powerful arms to drain the pits and to raise the coals, they call into employment multitudes of miners, engineers, ship-builders and sailors, and cause the construction of canals and railways; and, while they enable these rich fields of industry to be cultivated to the utmost, they leave thousands of fine arable fields free for the production of food to man, which must otherwise have been allotted to the food of horses. Steam engines, moreover, by the cheapness and steadiness of their action, fabricate cheap goods, and procure in their exchange a liberal supply of the necessaries and comforts of life, produced in foreign lands. . . .

The steam engine is, in fact, the controller general and main-spring of British industry, which urges it onwards at a steady rate, and never suffers it to lag or loiter, till its appointed task be done.

The steam loom, introduced into England in the early 1820s and shortly thereafter in the United States, revolutionized textile production. It wove seven times as much cloth as the hand loom, and employers rushed to replace male hand-loom weavers by machines. Richard Guest, an English economist, discussed the extraordinary advantages of steam in weaving in the 1823 *Compendius History of Cotton-Manufacture*. Thousands of hand-loom weavers in England lost their jobs in the coming years as a result of this invention. Eventually they too would wind up in the factory.

The same powerful agent which so materially forwarded and advanced the progress of the Cotton Manufacture in the concluding part of the last century, has lately been further used as a substitute for manual labour, and the Steam Engine is now applied to the working of the loom as well as to the preparatory processes. . . .

It is a curious circumstance, that, when the Cotton Manufacture was in its infancy, all the operations, from the dressing of the raw material to its being finally turned out in the state of cloth, were completed under the roof of the weaver's cottage. The course of improved manufacture which followed, was to spin the yarn in factories and to weave it in cottages. At the present time, when the manufacture has attained a mature growth, all the operations, with vastly increased means and more complex contrivances, are again performed in a single building. The Weaver's cottage with its rude apparatus of peg warping, hand cards, hand wheels, and imperfect looms, was the Steam Loom factory in miniature. Those vast brick edifices in the vicinity of all the great manufacturing towns in the south of Lancashire, towering to the height of seventy or eighty feet, which strike the attention and excite the curiosity of the traveller, now perform labours which formerly employed whole villages. In the Steam Loom factories, the cotton is carded, roved, spun, and woven into cloth, and the same quantum of labour is now performed in one of these structures which formerly occupied the industry of an entire district.

A very good Hand Weaver, a man twenty-five or thirty years of age, will weave two pieces of . . . shirting per week, each twenty-four yards long . . . A Steam Loom Weaver, fifteen years of age, will in the same time weave seven similar pieces. A Steam Loom factory containing two hundred Looms, with the assistance of one hundred persons under twenty years of age, and of twenty-five men, will weave seven hundred pieces per week, of the length and quality before described. To manufacture one hundred similar pieces per week by the hand, it would be necessary to employ at least one hundred and twenty-five Looms, because many of the Weavers are females, and have cooking, washing, cleaning and various other duties to perform; others of them are children and, consequently, unable to weave as much as the

A young woman factory worker shows off the steam-powered spinning frame used in American and English factories by the 1860s. This improvement over the spinning jenny produced more than thirty bobbins of thread simultaneously at a speed unattainable by a hand-operated machine.

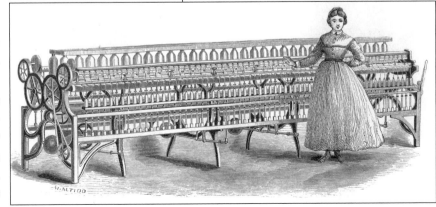

Two men in a British textile factory adjust the printing rollers and check the inks on large calico fabric printing machines. Calico was originally produced in the city of Calicut, India, and demand for this relatively cheap printed cotton cloth stimulated textile production in England.

men. It requires a man of mature age and a very good Weaver to weave two of the pieces in a week, and there is also an allowance to be made for sickness and other incidents. Thus, eight hundred and seventy-five hand Looms would be required to produce the seven hundred pieces per week; and reckoning the weavers, with their children, and the aged and infirm belonging to them at two and a half to each loom, it may very safely be said, that the work done in a Steam Factory containing two hundred Looms, would, if done by hand Weavers, find employment and support for a population of more than two thousand persons.

The French followed the British in applying steam power to all forms of manufacture. In 1867, Bernard Samuelson, a British member of Parliament, visited the Creusot ironworks in France, and described the forge and the system of training that supported it in a letter to the Vice President of the Parliamentary Committee of Council on Education.

The [Le Creusot] works . . . now cover 300 acres; the workshops and forges 50 acres; and the mines yield annually 250,000 tons of coal, and 300,000 tons of iron ore; 300,000 tons of coal and about 120,000 tons of iron ore are purchased. The iron works produce more than 100,000 tons of iron, besides machinery, locomotive and marine, iron bridges and viaducts, and even iron gunboats and river steamers. . . . These marvelous works have therefore been virtually created in 30 years and in fact the well-built, well-paved town of Creusot, with its churches, its schools, its markets, its gas and water works, and its handsome public walks, inhabited by nearly 24,000 well-fed and decently-clad people, has taken the place of the wretched pit-village of 2,700 inhabitants of 1836. . . .

[T]he new forge, contained under a single roof . . . is probably unequalled in the world. A very large proportion of the personnel of every rank in this great establishment was born and has been trained on the spot, and the possibility of thus forming highly skilled workmen, competent engineers and accountants, is due in great measure to a system of education dating back as far as 1841, which, though it is modestly styled elementary, is far more advanced and "special" than the term implies. . . . Education is not compulsory, but no Creusot boy is admitted into the works who cannot read and write, and none who has been turned out of the school for misbehavior. . . . Of late years, 6 of the heads of departments, pupils of the Ecole des Arts et Métiers [School of Arts and Trades], have been appointed to teach special classes, bearing directly on the occupations of the workmen.

Race and Gender

In order for the industrial revolution to occur, manufacturers needed raw materials such as cotton, produced by slave labor on the plantations of the southern United States. American cotton was crucial to the growth of the British and American textile industries. In the narrative of his life, former slave Solomon Northup described the brutal experience of working on an American cotton plantation in the early 1850s, producing the raw material of early industrialization. Even though the British abolished the slave trade in 1807, and the United States forbade Southern planters to trade in slaves the same year, slavery persisted for another fifty-six years. Once the Civil War ended, slavery and the plantation system collapsed in the United States, and British manufacturers turned to Egypt and India for raw materials, thus expanding the global reach of the industrial economy.

In the latter part of August begins the cotton-picking season. At this time each slave is presented with a sack. . . . [E]ach one is also presented with a large basket that will hold about two barrels. This is to put the cotton in when the sack is filled. . . .

Picking cotton in the American South was backbreaking work that employed African American women and children for decades after the Civil War. Their labor fueled the textile industries of Britain and New England.

When a new hand . . . is sent for the first time into the field, he is whipped up smartly, and made for that day to pick as fast as he can possibly. At night it is weighed, so that his capability in cotton picking is known. He must bring in the same weight each night following. If it falls short, it is considered evidence that he has been laggard, and a greater or less number of lashes is the penalty. . . .

The hands are required to be in the cotton fields as soon as it is light in the morning, and, with the exception of ten or fifteen minutes which is given them at noon to swallow their allowance of cold bacon, they are not permitted to be a moment idle until it is too dark to see. . . .

The day's work over in the field, the baskets are "toted" . . . to the gin-house, where the cotton is weighed. . . . A slave never approaches the gin-house with his basket of cotton but with fear. If it falls short in weight . . . he knows that he must suffer. And if he has exceeded it by ten or twenty pounds, in all probability his master will measure the next day's task, accordingly. . . . After weighing, follow the whippings; and then the baskets are carried to the cotton house and their contents stored away like hay, all hands being sent in to tramp it down. . . .

This done, the labor of the day is not yet ended, by any means. Each one must then attend to his respective chores. One feeds the mules, another the swine, another cuts the wood and so forth. . . . Finally, at a late hour, they reach the quarters, sleepy and overcome with the long day's toil. Then a fire must be kindled in the cabin, the corn ground in the small hand-mill, and supper, and dinner for the next day in the field, prepared. All that is allowed them is corn and bacon, which is given out at the corncrib and smokehouse every Sunday morning. Each one receives, as his weekly allowance, three and a half pounds of bacon, and corn enough to make a peck of meal. That is all. . . .

The same fear of punishment with which [the slaves] approach the gin-house, possesses them again on lying down to get a snatch of rest. It is the fear of oversleeping in the morning. Such an offence would certainly be attended with not less than twenty lashes. With a prayer that he may be on his feet and wide awake at the first sound of the horn, he sinks to his slumbers nightly.

Cotton grown by slaves in the American South fueled the industrial revolution. In the United States, beginning in the last decade of the eighteenth century, textile factories sprang up along rivers throughout New England. In 1790, Samuel Slater opened a small mill in Pawtucket, Rhode Island. In the early 1800s, Francis Cabot Lowell's large factory on the banks of the Merrimack River in Massachusetts employed young women and girls from the surrounding countryside. Employers believed that young women would be obedient workers and that they could pay them less than men. The young girls who worked in the Lowell mills wrote letters home to friends and family. Written in the 1840s, the letters give historians valuable insights about factory life. This letter, written by a girl named Susan in 1844, described the factory experience as a decidedly mixed one.

Lowell, April [1844].
Dear Mary: In my last I told you I would write again, and say more of my life here; and this I will now attempt to do.

I went into the mill to work a few days after I wrote to you. It looked very pleasant at first, the rooms were so light, spacious, and clean, the girls so pretty and neatly dressed, and the machinery so brightly polished or nicely painted. The plants in the windows, or on the overseer's bench or desk, gave a pleasant aspect to things. You will wish to know what work I am doing. I will tell you of the different kinds of work.

There is, first, the carding-room, where the cotton flies most, and the girls get the dirtiest. But this is easy, and the females are allowed time to go out at night before the bell rings—on Saturday night at least, if not on all other nights. Then there is the spinning

Factory owners subsidized the publication of the Lowell Offering, *a monthly magazine written by the women working in the textile mills of Lowell, Massachusetts. On the cover of this issue, a young girl carries a book as a reminder that the mill owners encouraged factory girls to improve themselves by reading. The beehive on her left is a symbol of industrious activity.*

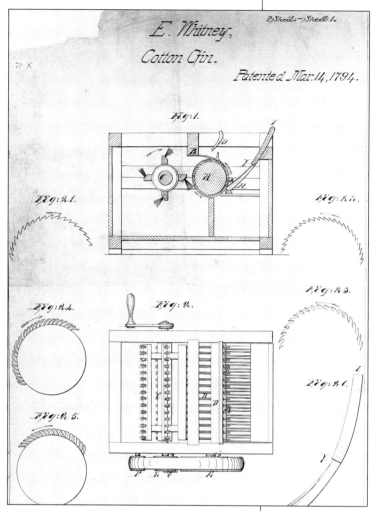

American inventor Eli Whitney patented his cotton gin in March 1794. The "gin," short for engine, used a system of spiked rollers, turned by a hand crank, to remove the seeds from cotton. It revolutionized cotton production by speeding up the preparation of cotton for spinning.

room, which is very neat and pretty. In this room are the spinners and doffers. The spinners watch the frames; keep them clean, and the threads mended if they break. The doffers take off the full bobbins, and put on the empty ones . . . . [Weavers] have the hardest time of all—or can have, if they choose to take charge of three or four looms, instead of the one pair which is the allotment. . . .

I could have had work in the dressing-room, but chose to be a weaver; and I will tell you why. I disliked the closer air of the dressing-room, though I might have become accustomed to that. I could not learn to dress so quickly as I could to weave, nor have work of my own so soon, and should have had to stay with Mrs. C. two or three weeks before I could go in at all, and I did not like to be "lying on my oars" so long. And, more than this, when I get well learned I can have extra work, and make double wages, which you know is quite an inducement with some.

[When] I went into the mill . . . [at] first the hours seemed very long, but I was so interested in learning that I endured it very well; and when I went out at night the sound of the mill was in my ears, as of crickets, frogs, and jewsharps, all mingled together in strange discord. After that it seemed as though cotton-wool was in my ears, but now I do not mind at all. You know that people learn to sleep with the thunder of Niagara in their ears and a cotton mill is no worse, though you wonder that we do not have to hold our breath in such a noise.

It makes my feet ache and swell to stand so much . . . The girls generally wear old shoes about their work . . . but they almost all say that when they have worked here a year or two they have to procure shoes a size or two larger than before they came. The right hand, which is the one used in stopping and starting the loom becomes larger than the left; but in other respects the factory is not detrimental to a young girl's appearance. . . .

You wish to know . . . of our hours of labor. We go in at five o'clock; at seven we come out to breakfast; at half-past seven we return to our work, and stay until half-past twelve. At one, or quarter-past one four months in the year, we return to our work, and stay until seven at night. Then the evening is all our own, which is more than some laboring girls can say, who think nothing is more tedious.

In 1859, French writer Louis Reybaud published a study of the conditions of workers in the silk industry. Reybaud was struck by the predominating role of women, who made up the majority of workers in silk production. His account suggests that although employers valued certain qualities in women, they also believed in stereotypical views of the differences between the sexes. They viewed women as more docile, more easily disciplined, and willing to work for lower wages than men. Reybaud's observations also show that, as late as the 1850s, many European families combined agricultural and industrial activities.

Even [in rural areas] where large farms prevail, industrial activity persists; there is always room somewhere for two or three looms. Not a single rural family would deprive itself of this supplement to income. Tasks are merely distributed according to strength and aptitude. Strong and vigorous men go out to the fields to plant and cultivate, while women and adolescents remain at home to weave velvet and taffeta. Nor is this division of labor a local or circumscribed phenomenon; I have found the same thing in all areas of rural manufacture: in Prussia as in Switzerland . . . [in France] in the areas around Saint Etienne and Lyon. Except for work that requires physical strength, silk weaving tends to pass out of the hands of men into the hands of women. Women are employed in the vast majority of mechanized establishments; in towns and cities as well, there is a growing trend in this direction.

[As for the motives,] the main one is in the real economic advantage that results from this substitution [of women for men]; a man would never be happy with the wages that suffice for a woman. But this is not the only advantage. One finds qualities in the woman worker that are increasingly rare in the male worker: sedentary habits, the spirit of discipline, exactitude at work, loyalty. Beyond that, a preference which was at first limited to simple fabrics has extended to the more complicated fabrics, without any noticeable inferiority in execution. What is lacking, in effect, in women, is neither intelligence, nor dexterity, on the contrary these are the best qualities of the [female] labor force. As for muscular strength, this is necessary only on the really wide looms and for special fabrics.

"If to exist, to procure a pittance of food and decent clothing, a young woman must toil incessantly at some handicraft from five years old and upwards, where and how is she to learn needlework, cookery, economy, cleanliness, and all the "arts of home?"

—Anna Jameson, *Memoirs and Essays Illustrative of Art, Literature, and Social Morals*, 1846.

Harsh Discipline and Awful Conditions

In factories in both Europe and America, strict rules governed daily routines, regulating workers' lives from sunup to sundown. In Berlin metalworking factories, workers who arrived late lost wages, and employers locked the doors after work began and subjected workers to an almost military regimentation. These work rules for men employed in the foundry and engineering works of the Royal Overseas Trading Co. in Moabit, Germany, in 1844 illustrate how nineteenth-century employers controlled their workers in order to extract the most labor in the most efficient way possible. Employers also tried to use workers to discipline each other.

[T]he following rules shall be strictly observed.

(1) The normal working day begins at all seasons at 6 A.M. precisely and ends, after the usual break of half an hour for breakfast, an hour for dinner and half an hour for tea, at 7 P.M., and it shall be strictly observed.

Five minutes before the beginning of the stated hours of work until their actual commencement, a bell shall ring and indicate that every worker employed in the concern has to proceed to his place of work, in order to start as soon as the bell stops.

The doorkeeper shall lock the door punctually at 6 A.M., 8.30 A.M., 1 P.M. and 4.30 P.M. . . .

(2) When the bell is rung to denote the end of the working day, every workman, both on piece- and on day-wage, shall leave his workshop and the yard, but is not allowed to make preparations for his departure before the bell rings. Every breach of this rule shall lead to a fine . . . Only those who have obtained special permission by the overseer may stay on in the workshop in order to work. If a workman has worked beyond the closing bell, he must give his name to the gatekeeper on leaving, on pain of losing his payment for the overtime.

(3) No workman, whether employed by time or piece, may leave before the end of the working day, without having first received permission from the overseer and having given his name to the gatekeeper. Omission of these two actions shall lead to a fine.

(4) Repeated irregular arrival at work shall lead to dismissal. This shall also apply to those who are found idling by an official or overseer, and refuse to obey their order to resume work.

So strict are the instructions that if an overseer of a room be found talking to any person in the mill during working hours he is dismissed immediately—two or more overseers are employed in each room, if one be found a yard out of his ground he is discharged . . . everyone, manager, overseers, mechanics, oilers, spreaders, spinners, and reelers, have their particular duty pointed out to them, and if they transgress, they are instantly turned off as unfit for their situation.

—Employee's description of the discipline at a British flax mill, *Information Regarding Flax Spinning at Leeds*, 1821

REGULATIONS

To be observed by all Persons employed by the

Proprietors of the Tremont Mills.

THE Overseers are to be punctually in their Rooms at the starting of the Mill, and not to be absent unnecessarily during working hours. They are to see that all those employed in their rooms are in their places in due season, and keep a correct account of their time and work. They may grant leave of absence to those employed under them when there are spare hands in the room to supply their places; otherwise they are not to grant leave of absence except in cases of absolute necessity.

All persons in the employ of the Proprietors of the Tremont Mills, are required to observe the regulations of the room where they are employed. They are not to be absent from their work without consent, except in case of sickness, and then they are to send the Overseer word of the cause of their absence.

They are to board in one of the Boarding houses belonging to the Company, and conform to the regulations of the house where they board.

The Company will not employ any one who is habitually absent from public worship on the Sabbath.

All persons entering into the employment of the Company are considered as engaging to work twelve months.

All persons intending to leave the employment of the Company are to give two week's notice of their intention to their Overseer; and their engagement with the Company is not considered as fulfilled, unless they comply with this regulation.

Payments will be made monthly, including board and wages, which will be made up to the last Saturday of every month, and paid in the course of the following week.

These Regulations are considered a part of the contract with all persons entering into the employment of the Proprietors of the TREMONT MILLS.

J. AIKEN, AGENT.

Mill owners posted the regulations of the Merrimack Manufacturing Company in Lowell, Massachusetts, to remind workers of the importance of factory discipline. Rules also applied to their conduct outside the factory.

(5) Entry to the firm's property by any but the designated gateway, and exit by any prohibited route, e.g. by climbing fences or walls, or by crossing the [River] Spree, shall be punished by a fine . . . for the first offences, and dismissal for the second.

(6) No worker may leave his place of work otherwise than for reasons connected with his work.

(7) All conversation with fellow-workers is prohibited; if any worker requires information about his work, he must turn to the overseer, or to the particular fellow-worker designated for the purpose.

(8) Smoking in the workshops or in the yard is prohibited during working hours; anyone caught smoking shall be fined . . . for every such offence.

(9) Every worker is responsible for cleaning up his space in the workshop, and if in doubt, he is to turn to his overseer. All tools must always be kept in good condition, and must be cleaned after use. This applies particularly to the turner, regarding his lathe.

(10) Natural functions must be performed at the appropriate places, and whoever is found soiling walls, fences, squares, etc., and similarly, whoever is found washing his face and hands in the workshop and not in the places assigned for the purpose, shall be fined . . .

(12) It goes without saying that all overseers and officials of the firm shall be obeyed without question, and shall be treated with due deference. Disobedience will be punished by dismissal.

(13) Immediate dismissal shall also be the fate of anyone found drunk in any of the workshops. . . .

(15) Every workman is obliged to report to his superiors any acts of dishonesty or embezzlement on the part of his fellow workmen.

Most factory conditions were terrible. Metalworkers worked with toxic materials; in spinning, the air was so damp that workers easily contracted respiratory infections. Until the end of the nineteenth century, workers toiled for a grueling thirteen to fourteen hours a day with only short periods for rest and meals. Such conditions were strikingly similar all over Europe and America. British journalist and politician William Cobbett published these observations in his journal the *Political Register* in November 1824. Cobbett compared factory workers in Britain to the condition of enslaved workers in the United States, but he believed that the conditions of industrial labor were even worse than the conditions of plantation slavery.

Some of these lords of the loom have in their employ thousands of miserable creatures. In the cotton-spinning work these creatures are kept, fourteen hours in each day, locked up, summer and winter, in a heat of from EIGHTY TO EIGHTY-FOUR DEGREES. . . .

Now, then, do you duly consider what a heat of eighty-two is? Very seldom do we feel such a heat as this in England. The 31st of last August, and the 1st, 2nd, and 3rd of last September, were

Steelworkers in a Pittsburgh foundry stand clear of the sparks and flames released into the air as molten metal is converted into steel. This new process of steel production, developed in England in the mid-1850s, made it possible to remove impurities from steel and make a stronger product, but the working conditions remained dangerous.

very hot days. The newspapers told us that men had dropped down dead in the harvest fields and that many horses had fallen dead upon the road; and yet the heat during those days never exceeded eighty-four degrees in the hottest part of the day. We were retreating to the coolest rooms in our houses; we were pulling off our coats, wiping the sweat off our faces, puffing, blowing, and panting; and yet we were living in a heat nothing like eighty degrees. What, then, must be the situation of the poor creatures who are doomed to toil, day after day, for three hundred and thirteen days in the year, fourteen hours in each day, in an average heat of eighty-two degrees? Can any man, with a heart in his body, and a tongue in his head, refrain from cursing a system that produces such slavery and such cruelty?

Observe, too, that these poor creatures have no cool room to retreat to, not a moment to wipe off the sweat, and not a breath of air to come and interpose itself between them and infection.

The door of the place wherein they work, is *locked*, except *half an hour*, at tea-time; the workpeople are not allowed to send for water to drink, in the hot factory; even the *rain-water is locked* up, by the master's order, otherwise they would be happy to drink even that. If any spinner be found with his *window open*, he is to pay a fine of a shilling! Mr. Martin of Galway has procured Acts of Parliament to be passed to prevent *cruelty to animals*. If horses or dogs were shut up in a place like this they would certainly be thought worthy of Mr. Martin's attention.

Not only is there not a breath of sweet air in these truly infernal scenes; but, for a large part of the time, there is the abominable and pernicious stink of the GAS to assist in the murderous effects of the heat. In addition to the heat and the gas; in addition to the noxious effluvia of the gas, mixed with the steam, there are the *dust*, and what is called the *cotton-flyings* or fuzz, which the unfortunate creatures have to inhale; and the fact is, the notorious fact is, that well-constitutioned men are rendered old and past labour at forty years of age, and that children are rendered decrepit and deformed, and thousands upon thousands of them slaughtered by consumptions, before they arrive at the age of sixteen. And are these establishments to boast of? If we were to admit the fact they compose an addition to the population of the country; if we were further to admit that they caused an addition to the pecuniary resources of the Government, ought not a government to be ashamed to derive resources from such means?

The French novelist Emile Zola was outraged by the conditions of French mine workers. Although the French government passed legislation in 1874 forbidding women and children to work underground in mines, many continued to do so. In his novel *Germinal*, published in 1885, Zola described the work of two young mine workers, Etienne and Catherine, who worked in the mine shaft pushing loaded tubs of coal to the surface. Zola based the novel on the Le Creusot coal mines in south central France, where workers struck for higher wages and shorter hours in 1870.

Etienne, whose eyes were getting used to the darkness, looked at Catherine . . . he was amazed by the strength and speed of the child, which was based more on skill than on muscle. She filled her tub quicker than he could, with short, quick, regular thrusts of her shovel; she then pushed it up to the incline, with one long, smooth movement, slipping effortlessly under the overhanging

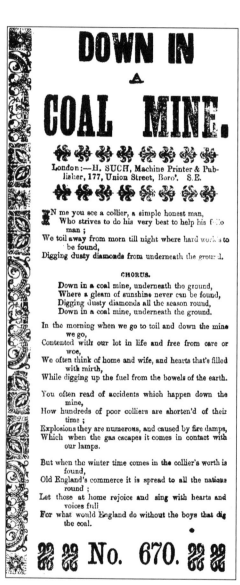

English miners' songs often described the grim dangers that awaited them underground and also served as social and political commentary. The author of this song commented ironically on the fact that miners' dangerous work provided warmth to English homes in winter and boosted England's overseas trade.

A young girl, naked to the waist and strapped by a harness to a coal wagon, pulls it to the surface of the coal pit. This engraving, made for the British Parliament's inquiry into conditions in the mines in 1842, was designed to expose the evils of child labor.

rocks . . . [while] he kept banging and scraping himself, crashing his tub and grinding to a halt.

To tell the truth, it certainly wasn't an easy trip. The distance from the coal face to the incline was fifty or sixty metres; and the passage, which the stonemen had not yet widened, was hardly more than a gully, whose very uneven roof bulged and buckled all over the place: in some places there was only just enough room to get the loaded tub through. [They] had to crouch and push on hands and knees to avoid splitting their heads open. Besides, the props had already started to bend and split. You could see long pale cracks running right up the middle of them, making them look like broken crutches. You had to watch out not to rip your skin on these splinters; and under the relentless pressure, which was slowly crushing these oak posts even though they were as thick as a man's thigh, you had to slip along on your belly, with the secret fear of suddenly hearing your back snap in two.

She had to show him how to walk with his legs apart, bracing his feet against the timbers on either side of the tunnel in order to get some solid leverage. His body should be bent forward, and his arms stretched out straight in front of him so as to use all his muscles, including those of his shoulders and hips. He spent one whole trip following her, watching her run . . . with her hands placed so low she seemed to be trotting on all fours, like some small circus animal. She sweated and panted, and her joints were creaking, but she didn't complain, displaying the dull acceptance acquired by habit, as if it were mankind's common lot to live in this wretched, prostrate condition. But he was unable to follow her example, for his shoes hurt, and his body ached, from walking in that position with his head bent down. After a few minutes, the position became clear torture, an intolerable anguish so painful that he had to stop and kneel down for a moment so as to straighten his back and breathe freely.

Chapter Three: Picture Essay

A Childhood at Work

Child labor existed virtually everywhere that industrial capitalism flourished. In America as well as in Europe, children as young as five years of age labored in the textile and carpet factories, mines, glassworks, and garment-making sweatshops. Others worked at home making artificial flowers, shelling walnuts, or sewing clothes. During the 1820s, children under sixteen made up almost half of the cotton textile workers in the United States. Employers eagerly hired children for many of the same reasons that they employed women: children's small fingers enabled them to sew and to knot carpets effectively; they could easily get under machines to fix broken threads; their small bodies enabled them to work in narrow mine shafts. Employers believed they could pay them much less than adults and that children would be pliant and submissive workers. Abuse of children was common. Employers routinely beat and otherwise physically abused their small employees, who were powerless to defend themselves. Children also experienced the same health hazards on the job as adults, but at very young ages.

From the early nineteenth century on, painters depicted child labor to bring this practice to the public's attention and as a form of social criticism. But paintings that hung in museums and in the homes of the wealthy reached only a limited audience. Engraving, a process that had been used for centuries, made images accessible to a larger public in newspapers and broadsides hawked on the streets. In the 1830s, the new medium of photography realistically documented children's participation in the industrial revolution.

Despite numerous efforts to stop child labor, areas of England, continental Europe, and the United States still tolerated it well into the twentieth century. Not until 1916 did the U.S. Congress pass the first federal legislation prohibiting the employment of children, but this law was not enforced until the 1930s. In the meantime, children continued to labor in often dangerous and unhealthy conditions. For most it was a rude awakening into adulthood.

A group of "breaker boys" who broke up coal in the Woodward Coal Mines of Kingston, Pennsylvania, around 1900. Perhaps as young as nine or ten, the boys wear overalls or trousers and jackets, as well as caps to keep the coal dust out of their hair. Photographed at the end of the day, their faces are covered with coal dust. Most people in the United States had no inkling of the desperate poverty that drove parents to send their young boys into the mines.

In this detail from a 1770s painting, two girls sew dresses under the direction of an adult woman in a small dressmaking workshop in France. The products of their labors hang on hooks above their heads. At the same time that Britain experienced an industrial revolution, small garment-making workshops like this one flourished all over Europe.

A large crowd of laborers leave work at the end of the day in this 1868 engraving. The artist placed a group of small boys right in the center of the engraving, making it clear that children were very much a part of the factory labor force. Everyone carries a lunch pail or basket, for workers had to bring their own meals to work. An imposing brick factory—their place of work—looms in the distance.

A barefoot little boy in London sells matches from a wooden box strapped to his neck in this 1884 photograph. The box reads "Bryant and May's," one of the largest manufacturers of matches in England. Selling manufactured goods on the streets of large cities such as London was a common form of child labor during the industrial revolution.

A postcard from the end of the nineteenth century shows women and young girls of seven or eight employed in a silk spinning factory near Aubenas, in the Cévennes Mountains in southern France. Their job was to plunge raw silk cocoons into boiling water in order to separate the silk fibers. The factory appears to be lit by daylight streaming in through the skylight and the open windows. In these cramped conditions, it must have been incredibly hot, especially in summer.

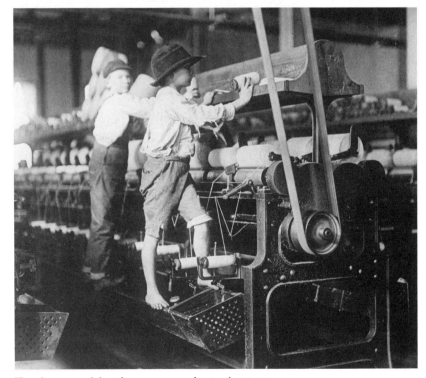

Two boys stand barefoot on a mechanized spinning frame in a textile factory in Macon, Georgia, in 1909. The boys' job was to pull off the finished bobbins, drop them into the metal basket at the bottom of the machine, and replace them with empty bobbins. Both boys appear almost dwarfed by the size of the machines.

Two young boys work in the Cumberland glass-works in Bridgeton, New Jersey, in 1909. Their job was to work for hours at a time holding the molds into which experienced adult glass blowers blew the molten glass. The workshop is cramped and relatively dark.

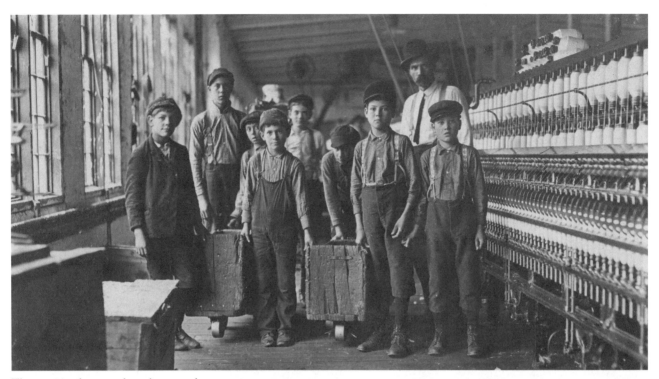

This 1908 photograph, taken in the Catawba Cotton Mill in Newton, North Carolina, shows a group of boys who took finished bobbins from the spinning machines and brought them to the weavers. A large mechanized spinning frame stands at the right of the picture. The youngest boy looks to be nine or ten years old. The man with the mustache and the hat, the superintendent, towers over them. The cotton dust on the floor filled the air—and workers' lungs—when the machines were running. Children as well as adult workers suffered severe respiratory problems, today known as white lung disease.

A *Chicago Daily News* photographer snapped this image of girls sitting at a sewing table in Chicago, Illinois, in about 1903. The photograph was taken during a sweatshop inspection by labor inspectors. The girls are sewing men's suit jackets by hand. In the background several men work at other tasks. The gender division of labor was common in this industry.

Young girls participate in a May Day labor parade in New York City on May 1, 1909. The two girls in the front wear banners that read "Abolish Child Slavery" in both English and Yiddish, the language spoken by the hundreds of Eastern European Jewish women and children who worked in the New York garment industry.

Chapter Four

The Family and Private Life in the Industrial Age

The enormous changes the industrial revolution brought to Europe and North America profoundly affected men's and women's family lives. Many men, women, and children left farms and family workshops and joined the ranks of industrial labor, working apart from one another in large factories often located some distance from home. Differences also appeared between families. Everywhere, the industrial revolutions created two social classes: the middle-class owners of factories, banks, and shipping companies; and the working class that provided the manual labor. Although middle-class men and women reaped the profits and benefits of industrial growth, these profits rarely touched the lives of workers. The private family lives of working people and their middle-class employers reflected this difference between the classes.

During the course of the nineteenth century, writers and social observers in both Europe and America responded to the tremendous social changes of the period by paying special attention to the relations between men and women in public and private life. The belief that men and women were destined to "separate spheres"—that men belonged in the public sphere of work and politics, whereas women belonged in the private sphere of the home and family—gained ground. This view of the world of course neglected the fact that many women had to work for their families' economic survival. Some writers—of both the middle class and the working class—even argued for the desirability of paying working men a "family wage," in order that

their wives and children would not have to work for wages and might remain at home. Others instructed middle-class women to devote themselves to caring for their children and families and to cultivate domestic skills such as making jam or embroidering doilies for their living-room furniture. By not working outside of the home, women could serve as the living symbols of their husbands' prosperity. Contemporary observers also believed that separating the activities of men and women in this way could bring social peace to a society that increasingly teemed with dirt, immorality, and disorder. Yet, the ideal of "separate spheres"—separating men's work and women's work—failed to depict the reality of the lives of men and women of both classes, even if it helped to shape them.

In real life, public and private domains intersected with each other in multiple ways. Middle-class women regularly entered the public sphere of work, politics, and social reform. In Britain and the United States, for example, many became antislavery activists in the 1830s and 1840s; others worked to reform working-class women who had "fallen" into prostitution. Within the working class, the ideal of the housewife likewise failed to reflect the reality of family life, and the links between home and workplace often blurred. At the same time as factories began to move much production out of the domestic arena, small-scale manufacturing continued to flourish at home, especially in the garment and luxury trades. Throughout New York City, and in similar settings in Berlin and Paris, industries such as clothing and cigar manufacture employed numerous immigrant workers in cramped apartment buildings called tenements. These workers' children took part in production as well: for many, wage earning was a family affair. In order to avoid extra production costs during periods of economic slowdown, employers paid workers to labor at home, paying them only for what they produced, rather than an hourly wage.

At the same time, even if the ideal of "separate spheres" failed to reflect the reality of people's lives, it nonetheless had tremendous power to shape their lives. It influenced thinking about men and women's relation to the economy in both classes and significantly influenced women's wages and job opportunities. Employers (in some cases, pressured by male workers), convinced that women were really destined for a life of family, reproduction, and domesticity, believed that women only worked to supplement men's earnings. They therefore persisted in paying women less than men, often for the same work. The belief that women were more delicate and weaker than men also bolstered employers' dogged commitment to keeping men's and women's work separate and denying women access to opportunities for advancement and skilled jobs, which they reserved for men.

In the end, although the middle class and working class lived very differently, the classes intersected constantly. As the wealth of the middle class increased, prosperous middle-class families employed servants to cook, clean, and care for their children. The working-class women who took these jobs participated in the private and intimate lives of their employers on a daily basis: helping them dress, cleaning their clothes, caring for their children, and nursing them when sick. Indeed, the labor of working-class women and men enabled middle-class men and women to enjoy lives of relative leisure and to engage in reform activities or intellectual pursuits. The middle class clearly prospered; the working-class standard of living was another matter.

Historians continue to debate the effects of industrialization on the living standards of working-class families. Some have emphasized the long hours and unhealthy working conditions and the adverse effects on family life, not to mention childbearing and maternity. Workers rarely had leisure time with

A poster for a bicycle company features a woman enjoying a bicycle ride, an activity increasingly available to English middle-class women around the end of the nineteenth century. The industrial revolution led not only to more leisure time for the middle class, but also the production of more goods with which to enjoy that time, including mass-produced bicycles.

their families, and unsafe and unhealthy working conditions caused many women to die in childbirth. Poor nutrition, they claim, made workers weak and especially vulnerable to infections and disease. Yet, others have argued that the availability of more cheaply made mass consumption goods such as clothing and furniture improved workers' living standards and that workers' diets actually improved over the course of the nineteenth century. Whereas some have emphasized the cramped and dirty housing conditions of urban industrial workers, others have viewed positively the actions of a few employers in Britain and France who built housing for their labor force. Of course, much depends on how one measures the standard of living. Wages, food consumption, living space, and home ownership (as opposed to renting) are all factors, as is the availability of health care. Most agree that workers' lives did improve over the course of the nineteenth century: their wages rose, they ate better, enjoyed better housing, and were able to consume more of the very goods they spent their lives producing. But social class differences nonetheless remained strikingly apparent in family life.

Middle-Class Ideals

In both Europe and America, an explosion of advice and etiquette books and treatises on domestic economy popularized the middle-class ideal of women as the guardians of home and hearth. John Ruskin, a nineteenth-century English art critic, essayist, and lecturer defined the separate characters and spheres of the men and women in the industrial age in a lecture he gave in 1865.

Now their separate characters are briefly these. The man's power is active, progressive, defensive. He is eminently the doer, the creator, the discoverer, the defender. His intellect is for speculation and invention; his energy for adventure, for war, and for conquest, wherever war is just, wherever conquest necessary. But the woman's power is for rule, not for battle, and her intellect is not for invention or creation, but for sweet ordering, arrangement, and decision. She sees the qualities of things, their claims and their places. Her great function is Praise: she enters into no concert, but infallibly judges the crown of contest. By her office, and place, she is protected from all danger and temptation. The man, in his rough work in the open world, must encounter all peril and trial; to him, therefore, the failure, the offence, the inevitable error: often he must be wounded, or subdued, often misled, and always hardened. But he guards the woman from all this; within his house, as ruled by her, unless she herself has sought it, need enter no danger, no temptation, no cause of error or offence. This is the true nature of home—it is the place of Peace; the shelter, not only from all injury, but from all terror, doubt, and division. In so far as it is not this, it is not home; so far as the anxieties of the outer life penetrate into it, and the inconsistently-minded, unknown, unloved, or hostile society of the outer world is allowed by either husband or wife to cross the threshold, it ceases to be home; it is then only a part of the outer world which you have roofed over, and lighted fire in. But so far as it is a sacred place, a vestal temple, a temple of the hearth watched over by Household Gods, before whose faces none may come but those whom they can receive with love, so far as it is this, and roof and fire are types only of a nobler shade and light—shade as of the rock in a weary land, and light as of the Pharos in the stormy sea—so far it vindicated the name, and fulfils the praise, of home.

And wherever a true wife comes, this home is always round her. The stars only may be over her head; the glow worm in the night-cold grass may be the only fire at her foot: but home is yet wherever she is; and for a noblewoman it stretches far round her, better than ceiled with cedar, or painted with vermilion, shedding its quiet light far, for those who else were homeless.

An American, the Reverend Rufus William Bailey outlined the foundation of masculine authority in the household in his 1837 advice book. Bailey's book showed how nineteenth-century writers viewed the power relations between men and women in the well-ordered middle-class household in the period of industrialization.

The husband and wife are declared by the Maker to be one body. This was literally true in their "original" creation, where the man was first created of the dust of the earth, and then the woman formed out of the man. They are "one flesh," as they are the same kind of flesh in distinction from the lower animals. . . .

They are also one in a civil and a social sense. In the eye of law, and in their social relations, they have a community of goods. They mourn or rejoice together. Legally and morally, they can never be separated, but by an act, which forever renders the offending party unworthy of confidence in this relation, as it destroys in its nature the unity of the whole family economy. . . .

This ordinary-looking couple, photographed in 1861, is the very picture of middle-class respectability, which is exactly the impression they mean to convey. In fact, the couple is Queen Victoria of England and her husband, Prince Albert.

"Nothing should be thrown away so long as it is possible to make any use of it, however trifling that use may be; and whatever the size of the family, every member should be employed either in earning or saving money."

—Lydia Maria Child,
The Frugal Housewife, 1829

To ease the difficulties which will daily attend on the intercourse of the husband and wife, great forbearance will be found to be absolutely necessary. This is principally demanded on the part of the husband. With the right to decide in disputed points, a prudent man will weigh well the opinions of his wife, and by avoiding angry replies, will seek to bring her assent, if not her judgement, to his deliberate decision. An angry reply will perhaps awaken resentment, and end in bitterness of feeling, where love ought ever to reign. The least it can do is to stir up grief, and plant a thorn in that bosom which ever lies open to the emotions he chooses, by his treatment, to awaken, either of joy or grief, of sympathy or sorrow. . . .

Let the husband take care not to *play the tyrant* in his family. He is physically, and by a natural constitution, the strongest, and is set at the head of his family as a minister for good to those who are placed under his protection. If he indulges in ill temper, he will be very liable to abuse that power and become a tyrant in the exercise of it. A tyrant is the same in character, whether seated on a throne, or ruling with severity in his family; with this difference only, that the moral turpitude is greatest in the last case where the current of the affections is strongest, and moral susceptibilities are most quick. The political tyrant is often the best of husbands, but a tyrannical husband would be a tyrant everywhere. He, who can abuse his power in this relation, could hardly be entrusted with it in higher relations.

In 1861, an English expert on household management, Isabella Beeton published a book with helpful advice for middle-class wives about shopping, hiring and managing servants, housecleaning, and keeping account books. Although historians do not know whether women followed all of Beeton's advice, the book is a valuable source because of its prescriptions for the ideal domestic life. Beeton's book suggested anything but idle leisure for the middle-class wife. Paying strict attention to the details of household management would have kept her on her toes.

As with the commander of an army, or the leader of an enterprise, so is it with the mistress of a house. Her spirit will be seen through the whole establishment; and just in proportion as she performs her duties intelligently and thoroughly, so will her domestics follow in her path. Of all those acquirements, which more particularly belong to the feminine character, there are none which take a higher rank, in our estimation, than such as enter into a knowledge of household duties; for on these are perpetually dependent the happiness, comfort, and well-being of a family. . . .

Frugality and economy are home virtues, without which no household can prosper. . . . The necessity of practising economy should be evident to every one, whether in the possession of an income no more than sufficient for a family's requirements, or of a large fortune which puts financial adversity out of the question. . . .

In marketing, that the best articles are the cheapest, may be laid down as a rule; and it is desirable, unless an experienced and confidential housekeeper be kept, that the mistress should herself purchase all provisions and stores needed for the house. . . . A housekeeping account book should invariably be kept, and kept punctually and precisely. The plan for keeping household accounts, which we should recommend, would be to enter, that is, write down in a daily diary every amount paid on each particular day, be it ever so small; then, at the end of a week or a month, let these various payments be ranged under their specific heads of Butcher, Baker, &c.; and thus will be seen the proportions paid to each tradesman, and any week's or month's expenses may be contrasted with another. The housekeeping accounts should be balanced not less than once a month— once a week is better; and it should be seen that the money in hand tallies with the account. . . . Once a month it is advisable that the mistress overlook her store of glass and china, marking any breakages on the inventory of these articles.

When, in a large establishment, a housekeeper is kept, it will be advisable to examine her accounts regularly. Then, any increase of expenditure which may be apparent can easily be explained, and the housekeeper will have the satisfaction of knowing whether her efforts to manage her department well and economically have been successful.

The treatment of servants is of the highest possible moment, as well to the mistress as to the domestics themselves. On the head of the house the latter will naturally fix their attention; and if they perceive that the mistress' conduct is regulated by high and correct principles, they will not fail to respect her. If, also, a benevolent desire is shown to promote their comfort, at the same time that a steady performance of their duty is exacted, then their respect will not be unmingled with affection, and well-principled servants will be still more solicitous to continue to deserve her favor. . . .

The Servant's Magazine, *published in nineteenth-century England, is an example of how the middle class attempted to teach proper manners and behavior to their domestic servants. The two women on the cover are nursery maids whose responsibility was to bathe and feed the children and to care for them throughout the day.*

Beeton believed that an efficient mistress of the household would divide tasks according to the seasons. In her *Book of Household Management*, she spelled out the household tasks for spring, summer, fall, and winter.

It will be useful for the mistress and housekeeper to know the best seasons for various occupations connected with household management; and we, accordingly, subjoin a few hints which we think will prove valuable. . . .

The spring is the usual period set apart for house cleaning, and removing all the dust which will necessarily, with the best of housewives, accumulate during the winter months from the smoke of the coal, oil, gas &c. This season is also well adapted for washing and bleaching linen, &c., as, the weather not being then too hot for the exertions necessary in washing counterpanes, blankets, and heavy things in general, the work is better and more easily done than in the intense heat of July, which month some recommend for these purposes. Winter curtains should be taken down, and replaced by the summer white ones; and furs and woollen cloths also carefully laid by. . . . Included, under the general description of housecleaning, must be understood, turning out all the nooks and corners of drawers, cupboards, lumber room, loft, &c., with a view to getting rid of all unnecessary articles, which only create dirt and attract vermin; sweeping of chimneys, taking up carpets, painting and whitewashing the kitchen and offices, papering rooms, when needed, and, generally speaking, the house putting on, with the approaching summer, a bright appearance and a new face, in unison with nature. Oranges should now be preserved, and orange wine made.

The summer will be found, . . . in consequence of the diminution of labor for the domestics, the best period for examining and repairing household linen. . . . In June and July, gooseberries, currants, raspberries, strawberries, and other summer fruits, should be preserved, and jams and jellies made. In July too, the making of walnut ketchup should be attended to, as the green walnuts will be approaching perfection for this purpose. . . .

In the early autumn, plums of various kinds are to be bottled and preserved, and jams and jellies made.

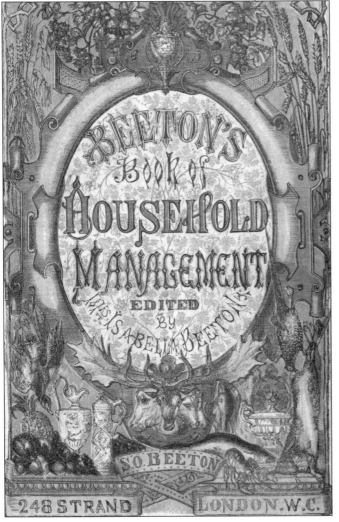

Isabella Beeton's Book of Household Management, *first published in 1861, sold hundreds of thousands of copies to women in England and America. It contained over two thousand recipes for everything from sauces and soups to fish, meat, chicken, and desserts, in addition to a wealth of advice about housekeeping.*

A little later, tomato sauce, a most useful article to have by you, may be prepared; a supply of apples laid in, if you have a place to keep them, as also a few keeping pears, and filberts. . . .

In September and October it will be necessary to prepare for the cold weather, and get ready the winter clothing for the various members of the family. The white summer curtains will now be carefully put away, the fireplaces, grates, and chimneys looked to, and the house put in a thorough state of repair, so that no "loose tile" may, at a future day, interfere with your comfort, and extract something considerable from your pocket.

In December, the principal household duty lies in preparing for the creature comforts of those near and dear to us, so as to meet Old Christmas with a happy face, a contented mind, and a full larder; and in storing the plums, washing the currants, cutting the citron, beating the eggs, and Mixing the Pudding, a housewife is not unworthily greeting the genial season of all good things.

Lydia Maria Child's strong opposition to slavery brought her into the antislavery movement in New England in the 1830s. In addition to combating slavery, she spoke out against crimes against Native Americans.

The domestic expectations for middle-class women meant that few were ladies of leisure. In her diary, American antislavery activist and writer Lydia Maria Child listed her activities during the year 1864. Although she came from the middle class, she did not have the luxury of relying on servants for many of her household activities. Some of her work included making items for Northern soldiers in the Civil War, then in progress, as well as for African-American freedwomen.

Wrote 235 letters.
Wrote 6 articles for newspapers.
Wrote 47 autograph articles for Fairs.
Wrote my Will.
Corrected Proofs for Sunset book.
Read aloud 6 pamphlets and 21 vollumes.
Read to myself 7 vollumes.
Made 25 needle books for Freedwomen.
2 Bivouac caps for soldiers.
Knit 2 pair of hospital socks.
Gathered and made peck of pickles for hospitals.
Knit 1 pair of socks for David.
Knit and made up 2 pairs of suspenders for D.
Knit six baby shirts for friends.
Knit 1 large Afghan & made the fringe.
Made 1 spectacle case for David.
Made 1 Door mat.

This illustration of cuts of meat from The Frugal Housewife, *written by Lydia Maria Child, a nineteenth-century American activist and writer, suggests that all animal parts except the head could be cooked and eaten. At a time when most domestic advice books were aimed at the upper classes, Child wrote advice for women without servants or even running water.*

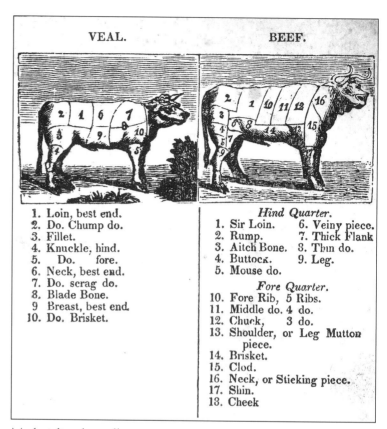

VEAL.

BEEF.

1. Loin, best end.
2. Do. Chump do.
3. Fillet.
4. Knuckle, hind.
5. Do. fore.
6. Neck, best end.
7. Do. scrag do.
8. Blade Bone.
9. Breast, best end.
10. Do. Brisket.

Hind Quarter.

1. Sir Loin.   6. Veiny piece.
2. Rump.   7. Thick Flank
3. Aitch Bone.   8. Thin do.
4. Buttock.   9. Leg.
5. Mouse do.

Fore Quarter.
10. Fore Rib, 5 Ribs.
11. Middle do. 4 do.
12. Chuck,   3 do.
13. Shoulder, or Leg Mutton
        piece.
14. Brisket.
15. Clod.
16. Neck, or Sticking piece.
17. Shin.
18. Cheek

Made 1 lined woollen cape.

Made 3 pair of corsets.

2 shirts for D.

1 Chemise.

2 flannel shirts for D.

Cut and made three gowns.

1 shirt with waist.

1 thick cotton petticoat.

1 quilted petticoat.

Made 1 silk gown.

Cut and made 1 Sac for myself.

Made double woollen dressing-gown for D.

1 pair of carpet-slippers for D.

Made 4 towels.

3 large lined curtains. 3 small ditto.

4 pillow cases.

New collars & wristbands to 6 shirts.

1 night cap.

1 pair of summer pantaloons.

Made a starred crib quilt, and quilted it; one fortnights work.

Spent 4 days collecting and sorting papers & pamphlets scattered by the fire.

Mended five pair of drawers.

Mended 70 pair of stockings.

Cooked 360 dinners.

Cooked 362 breakfasts.

Swept and dusted sitting-room & kitchen 350 times.

Filled lamps 362 times.

Swept and dusted chamber & stairs 40 times.

Besides innumerable jobs too small to be mentioned,

Preserved half a peck of barberries.

Made 5 visits to aged Women.

Tended upon invalid friend two days.

Made one day's visit to Medford and 3 visits to Boston; 2 of them for one day, the other for two days.

Made 7 calls upon neighbors.

Cut and dried half a peck of dried apples.

Working-Class Realities

The lifestyles of middle-class and working-class people could not have been more different. Although workers' neighborhoods might have been hidden from the gaze of those better off, social observers and reformers who chronicled the human effects of industrialization were appalled by the squalid conditions in which wForkers in industrial towns lived. Dr. Alphonse Guépin, a French medical doctor who treated the poor, described working-class housing in his book on the French city of Nantes in 1835.

If you want to know how [the worker] lives, go—for example—to the Rue des Fumiers which is almost entirely inhabited by this class of worker. Pass through one of the drain-like openings, below street-level, that lead to these filthy dwellings, but remember to stoop as you enter. One must have gone down into these alleys where the atmosphere is as damp and cold as a cellar; one must have known what it is like to feel one's foot slip on the polluted ground and to fear a stumble into the filth: to realise the painful impression that one receives on entering the homes of these unfortunate workers. Below street-level on each side of the passage there is a large gloomy cold room. Foul water oozes out of the walls. Air reaches the room through a sort of semi-circular

"It is a curious anomaly in the structure of modern society, that gentlemen may employ their hours of business in almost any degrading occupation and, if they have but the means of supporting a respectable establishment at home, may be gentlemen still; while, if a lady does but touch any article, no matter how delicate, in the way of trade, she loses caste and ceases to be a lady."

—Sarah S. Ellis, *The Women of England. Their Social Duties and Domestic Habits,* 1844

Illustrating class differences in French society, an upper-middle-class woman at the top of a pedestal gazes down at her social inferiors, who include a maid, a weaver, and a peasant woman to her right. On her left are a nun, a midwife, and a governess.

LES DIFFÉRENTES POSITIONS SOCIALES DE LA FEMME

window which is two feet high at its greatest elevation. Go in—if the fetid smell that assails you does not make you recoil. Take care, for the floor is uneven, unpaved and untiled—or if there are tiles, they are covered with so much dirt that they cannot be seen. And then you will see two or three rickety beds fitted to one side because the cords that bind them to the worm-eaten legs have themselves decayed. Look at the contents of the bed—a mattress; a tattered blanket of rags (seldom washed since there is only one); sheets sometimes; and a pillow sometimes. No wardrobes are needed in these homes. Often a weaver's loom and a spinning wheel complete the furniture. There is no fire in the winter. No sunlight penetrates [by day], while at night a tallow candle is lit. Here men work for fourteen hours [a day] for a daily wage of fifteen to twenty sous.

German workers were no better off. In 1845, economist and reformer Alexander Schneer interviewed city doctors as a way to investigate workers' housing, health, and morals in the German industrial city of Breslau. Some doctors believed that women's factory employment had a negative effect on workers' domestic life. Schneer's interviews show how governments began to take notice of how the industrial revolution contributed to poverty and poor living conditions.

Question: What is your usual experience regarding the cleanliness of these classes?

Dr. Bluemner: Bad! Mother has to go out to work, and can therefore pay little attention to the domestic economy, and even if she makes an effort, she lacks time and means. A typical woman of this kind has four children, of whom she is still suckling one, she has to look after the whole household, to take food to her husband at work, perhaps a quarter of a mile away on a building site; she therefore has no time for cleaning and then it is such a small hole inhabited by so many people. The children are left to themselves, crawl about the floor or in the streets, and are always dirty; they lack the necessary clothing to change more often, and there is no time or money to wash these frequently. There are, of course, gradations; if the mother is healthy, active and clean, and if the poverty is not too great, then things are better.

Question: What is the state of health among the lower classes ?

Dr. Bluemner: Since these classes are much more exposed to diseases, they usually are the first to be attacked by epidemic and sporadic disorders. Chronic rheumatism of the joints is a common illness, since they are constantly subject to colds. In addition, we find hernia with men, diseases of the reproductive organs with women because they have to start work only a few days after childbirth. Children mostly suffer from scrofula [a form of tuberculosis], which is almost general.

Dr. Neumann: . . . The very frequent incidence of anaemia among girls employed in factories deserves special mention. The hard work, the crowding of many individuals into closed rooms during their period of development, in which much exercise in the fresh air, plenty of sleep and only moderate exertion are most necessary, are sufficient explanation of this disease. The same condition also exists among the needlewomen, dressmakers, etc.

Dr. Kalckstein: . . . The dwellings of the working classes mostly face the yards and courts. The small quantity of fresh air admitted by the surrounding buildings is vitiated by the emanations from stables

Children stare out of an unpaved alley in the steel-producing town of Homestead, Pennsylvania, just after 1900. The badly maintained houses, opening onto an unpaved, garbage-strewn alley, were typical of the squalid conditions in which many working-class children grew up in American industrial towns.

Young men and women bend intently over their work making neckties in a New York tenement workshop around the turn of the twentieth century. Most likely they were paid piece rates—a sum for each necktie they produced—and had to work long hours to make a living wage.

Jacob Riis, American journalist and social investigator, wrote about and photographed working-class men, women, and children in New York City in the 1880s and 1890s. He published his writings and images in How the Other Half Lives *in 1890. This is how he described the smells and sights of an apartment workshop—a "tenement"—in Ludlow Street in New York's Lower East Side.*

Up two flights of dark stairs, three, four, with new smells of cabbage, of onions, of frying fish, on every landing, whirring sewing machines behind closed doors betraying what goes on within, to the door that opens to admit the bundle and the man. A sweater [one who works in a sweatshop] this, in a small way. Five men and a woman, two young girls, not fifteen and a boy who says unasked that he is fifteen, and lies in saying it, are at the machines sewing knickerbockers, "knee pants" in the Ludlow Street dialect. The floor is littered ankle-deep with half-sewn garments. In the alcove, on a couch of many dozens of "pants" ready for the finisher, a bare-legged baby with pinched face is asleep. A fence of piled-up clothing keeps him from rolling off on the floor. The faces, hands and arms to the elbows of everyone in the room are black with the color of the cloth on which they are working.

and middens [garbage heaps]. Further, because of the higher rents, people are forced to share their dwellings and to overcrowd them. How much the overcrowded living affects human health is shown by the experience on board ship, where at least cleanliness is always demanded, whereas among our labouring classes cleanliness is a very rare luxury. To this has to be added the fact that the poor population has to save its expensive fuel most carefully, so that they will not open windows or doors for any length of time in the cold season; these dwellings are therefore always filled with fetid air and steam, which condenses on the walls and creates green mould. The adults escape the worst influences by leaving the dwellings during the day, but the children are exposed to it with its whole force, for vitiated air interferes with the process of breathing, therefore does not clean the blood, so that this is inhibiting growth, and leads to scrofula and rickets.

Juggling Work and Family

In working-class families, all members, including children, contributed to wage earning. Most children worked in the days before compulsory primary education laws in the late nineteenth century required children to attend school. Jane Goode, a working-class mother of five, testified before the 1833 British Factory Commission investigating conditions in textile factories. Her account illustrates the importance of family in the household economy. Children who entered the

factory at age seven didn't have much of a childhood. Goode lost as many children as were still living.

I live at Old Radford, near Mr. Taylor's. I have had five children that have all worked at the factory. I have only one that works there now. She is sixteen. She works in the card-room. She minds the drawing-head. She gets 5 shillings 9 pence. She pays it all to me. She has worked there nine years. She has been at the drawing-head all the while. She got 2s. when she first went. She was just turned seven. All my other children are living. William is twenty-four next July. He is a soldier. He was 'twixt nine and ten when he went into the factory. It is seven years since he left. He never met any accident. None of them died. He is married now. Mary did not work here long. She went in about fourteen or fifteen. She was married last summer. She is thirty next June. She went on working at Elliot and Mill's and other factories till she married. Ann was just turned seven; she worked here four years, then she went to Mr. Elliot's, and worked there till she was mar-

REPORT OF ACCIDENT.—To Robert Baker, Esq., Inspector of Factories.

Name, Age, and Occupation of Person injured .. *Martha Appleton æt 13 a Scavenger*

Name of Firm, situation of the Factory in which the Accident occurred, and nature of the work carried on .... *Messrs William Woods Son Cotton Spinner Wallgate Wigan*

Date of Accident .... *Monday Aug 8th 1859*

Nature of Accident .... *Loss of all the fingers of the left hand*

Statement made to me by the injured person as to the cause of Accident, the hour of the day when it happened, and how that person was employed at the time .... *About 6.45 a.m. on Monday last I was at the back of the wheel house putting some bobbins in, when a giddiness came over me, and my hand slipped between the drawing and main douser wheels of the self acting mules.*

Martha Appleton was only thirteen years old when she lost all the fingers on her left hand in a work accident in a British factory. In this government factory inspector's report, Appleton describes a "giddiness" that came over her before her hand slipped into the machine. At the time of this report, in 1859, children older than twelve were still permitted to work ten hours a day, which could mean that Appleton's giddiness was actually exhaustion.

Betty Wardle described her experience of mine work to the 1842 British Parliamentary Commission investigating women's labor in the mines. Her testimony showed how private life and working life intersected in unexpected ways.

*B*etty Wardle, housewife, [from] Outwood, near Lever, was asked: Have you ever worked in a coal-pit? —Ay, I have worked in a pit since I was six years old.

Have you any children? —Yes. I have had four children; two of them were born while I worked in the pits.

Did you work in the pits while you were in the family way [pregnant]? —Ay, to be sure. I had a child born in the pits, and I brought it up the pitshaft in my skirt.

Are you sure that you are telling the truth? —Ay, that I am; it was born the day after I were married, that makes me to know.

Did you wear belt and chain [used to haul coal wagons up to the surface]? —Yes, sure I did.

ried, two years ago. She is nineteen next June. John was not eight when he went in; he is now twenty-two; it is about three years since he left. He lives at home, and works now with a twist machine [used to twist thread] at Lenton at George Staunton's. Hannah is sixteen. They have been all health, children; they have never ailed any thing, but it might be a cold, or what is common to all. I think when they do ail it is out of mismanagement, and not keeping them clean and comfortable. I have lived where I do now eleven or twelve years. My husband was a stockinger [stocking maker]. I seamed for him. There was not much for the children to do there. My eldest girl was in service then. I have had twelve children altogether. I thought you were asking only of those who worked at the mill. There were five that died before they were a quarter of a year old. Maria I had forgotten. She is married, and gone into Leicestershire. She was twelve when she began, and worked on till within these few weeks. She is twenty-seven nearly. She is married six or seven years . . . Jane is thirty-three. She worked at Derby mill two years. She was nineteen when she went. Mr. Samuel Wilson (now dead) came to Derby to get hands, and I engaged with him with my family. I did it to keep my children off the parish [welfare].

Given the long hours that most nineteenth-century workers labored, they had little time for leisure. Sunday was a day off almost everywhere, and in England, by the end of the nineteenth century, some employers allowed a half a day off on Saturday. But not until the early twentieth century did governments pass labor laws giving workers the eight-hour day. Writing about the rhythm of the workday in 1833 in his book, *The Manufacturing Population of England*, English surgeon Peter Gaskell suggested that industrial work corroded the relationship between family members.

The mode of life which the system of labour pursued in manufactories forces upon the operative, is one singularly unfavourable to domesticity.

Rising at or before day-break, between four and five o'clock the year round, scarcely refreshed by his night's repose, he swallows a hasty meal, or hurries to the mill without taking any food whatever. At eight o'clock half an hour, and in some instances forty minutes, are allowed for breakfast. In many cases, the engine continues at work during mealtime, obliging the labourer to eat and still overlook his work. This, however, is not universal. This meal is brought to the mill, and generally consists of weak tea, of course nearly cold, with a little bread; in other instances, of milk-and-meal porridge. Tea, however, may be called the universal breakfast, flavoured of late years too often with gin or other stimulants. . . . Where the hands live in immediate proximity to the mill,

TIME TABLE OF THE LOWELL MILLS,

Arranged to make the working time throughout the year average 11 hours per day.

TO TAKE EFFECT SEPTEMBER 21st., 1853.

The Standard time being that of the meridian of Lowell, as shown by the Regulator Clock of AMOS SANBORN, Post Office Corner, Central Street.

From March 20th to September 19th, inclusive.

COMMENCE WORK, at 6.30 A. M.   LEAVE OFF WORK, at 6.30 P. M., except on Saturday Evenings.
BREAKFAST at 6 A. M.   DINNER, at 12 M.   Commence Work, after dinner, 12.45 P. M.

From September 20th to March 19th, inclusive.

COMMENCE WORK at 7.00 A. M.   LEAVE OFF WORK, at 7.00 P. M., except on Saturday Evenings.
BREAKFAST at 6.30 A. M.   DINNER, at 12.30 P.M.   Commence Work, after dinner, 1.15 P. M.

BELLS.

From March 20th to September 19th, inclusive.

Morning Bells.	Dinner Bells.	Evening Bells.
First bell,..........4.30 A. M.	Ring out,.............12.00 M.	Ring out,............6.30 P. M.
Second, 5.30 A. M.; Third, 6.20.	Ring in,...........12.35 P. M.	Except on Saturday Evenings.

From September 20th to March 19th, inclusive.

Morning Bells.	Dinner Bells.	Evening Bells.
First bell,..........5.00 A. M.	Ring out,..........12.30 P. M.	Ring out at..........7.00 P. M.
Second, 6.00 A. M.; Third, 6.50.	Ring in,.............1.05 P. M.	Except on Saturday Evenings.

SATURDAY EVENING BELLS.

During APRIL, MAY, JUNE, JULY, and AUGUST, Ring Out, at 6.00 P. M.
The remaining Saturday Evenings in the year, ring out as follows :

SEPTEMBER.		NOVEMBER.		JANUARY.	
First Saturday, ring out 6.00 P. M.		Third Saturday ring out 4.00 P. M.		Third Saturday, ring out 4.25 P. M.	
Second " " 5.45 "		Fourth " " 3.55 "		Fourth " " 4.35 "	
Third " " 5.30 "					
Fourth " " 5.20 "		DECEMBER.		FEBRUARY.	
		First Saturday, ring out 3.50 P. M.		First Saturday, ring out 4.45 P. M.	
OCTOBER.		Second " " 3.55 "		Second " " 4.55 "	
First Saturday, ring out 5.05 P. M.		Third " " 3.55 "		Third " " 5.00 "	
Second " " 4.55 "		Fourth " " 4.00 "		Fourth " " 5.10 "	
Third " " 4.45 "		Fifth " " 4.00 "			
Fourth " " 4.35 "				MARCH.	
Fifth " " 4.25 "		JANUARY.		First Saturday, ring out 5.25 P. M.	
				Second " " 5.30 "	
NOVEMBER.		First Saturday, ring out 4.10 P. M.		Third " " 5.35 "	
First Saturday, ring out 4.15 P. M.		Second " " 4.15 "		Fourth " " 5.45 "	
Second " · " 4.05 "					

YARD GATES will be opened at the first stroke of the bells for entering or leaving the Mills.

.   *SPEED GATES commence hoisting three minutes before commencing work.*

This mill timetable from Lowell, Massachusetts, breaks down an eleven-hour workday, which began at 5:30 in the morning in spring and summer. Workers put in a six-day week, their time in the mill rigidly disciplined by the bells that marked off breakfast, the start of work, lunch (here referred to as "dinner") and the closing of the factory.

they visit home; but this rarely happens, as they are collected from all parts, some far, some near; but the majority too remote to leave the mill for that purpose. After this he is incessantly engaged—not a single minute of rest or relaxation being allowed him.

At twelve o'clock the engine stops, and an hour is given for dinner. The hands leave the mill, and seek their homes, where this meal is usually taken. It consists of potatoes boiled, very often eaten alone; sometimes with a little bacon, and sometimes with a portion of [meat]. This latter is, however, only found at the tables of the more provident and reputable workmen. If, as it often happens, the majority of the labourers reside at some distance, a great portion of the allotted time is necessarily taken up by the walk, or rather run, backwards and forwards. No time is allowed for the observances of ceremony. The meal has been imperfectly cooked, by some one left for that purpose. . . . The entire family surrounds the table, if they possess one, each striving which can most rapidly devour the miserable fare before them, which is sufficient, by its quantity, to satisfy the cravings of hunger, but possesses little nutritive quality. . . . As soon as this is [done], the family is again scattered. No rest has been taken; and even the exercise, such as it is, is useless, from its excess, and even harmful, being taken at a time when repose is necessary for the digestive operations.

Again they are closely [shut in the factory] from one o'clock till eight or nine, with the exception of twenty minutes . . . allowed for tea. . . . This imperfect meal is almost universally taken in the mill: it consists of tea and wheaten bread, with very few exceptions. During the whole of this long period they are actively and unremittingly engaged in a crowded room and an elevated temperature, so that, when finally dismissed for the day, they are exhausted equally in body and mind.

It must be remembered that father, mother, son and daughter, are alike engaged; no one capable of working is spared to make home (to which, after a day of such toil and privation, they are hastening) comfortable and desirable. No clean and tidy wife appears to welcome her husband—no smiling and affectionate mother to receive her children—no home, cheerful and inviting, to make it regarded. On the contrary, all assemble there equally jaded; it is miserably furnished—dirty and squalid in its appearance. Another meal, sometimes of a better quality, is now taken, and they either seek that repose which is so much needed, or leave home in pursuit of pleasure or amusements, which still further tend to increase the evils under which they unavoidably labour.

In his report to the British Parliament in 1845 on the workers of the city of Birmingham, England, R. A. Slaney, a member of Parliament, suggested that working-class women's lives were very different from the lives of middle-class women.

Amidst these scenes of wretchedness, the lot of the female sex is much the hardest. The man, if, as is usually the case, in employment, is taken away from the annoyances around his dwelling during the day, and is generally disposed to sleep soundly after his labours during the night; but the woman is obliged to remain constantly in the close court or neglected narrow alley where she lives, surrounded by all the evils adverted to; dirty children, domestic brawls, and drunken disputes meet her on every side and every hour. Under such circumstances the appropriate employments of a tidy housewife in brushing, washing, or cleansing, seem vain and useless efforts and she soon abandons them.

The task of holding onto a job and caring for young children could be daunting. Some working-class women in England and France resolved the dilemma of balancing work and child care by bringing their infants to work with them and drugging them with the liquid opiate laudanum, also known as Godfrey's cordial. An English druggist, "A. B.," testified about this practice before the English Parliamentary Children's Employment Commission of 1843. His observations also show how adults dealt with the stresses of their working lives. Those who did not dope themselves with laudanum probably handled the stress of daily life with a trip to the pub.

A mother looks adoringly at her smiling baby, who is enjoying the results of a product that soothed the gums of teething infants, but was actually mostly alcohol. Mothers often used such products to quiet their babies and let them get back to work.

Pharmacopoeia

A manual that listed recipes for common medications and their uses. Pharmacists relied on it for mixing and prescribing drugs.

A. B. He has been a chemist and druggist for many years in the town of Nottingham. A large quantity of laudanum and other preparations of opium, such as Godfrey's cordial, is sold by the chemists, especially in the poorer neighbourhoods of the town. He knows a chemist who sells as much as a gallon of laudanum a week in retail; and also knows that several chemists in Nottingham sell many gallons each in the year. A large quantity of solid opium is also sold; it is common, in many of the shops, to keep it ready prepared in small packets, like other articles in constant demand; these are sold at a penny or two pence each. The witness is obliged to prepare the laudanum of a greater strength than is prescribed in the *Pharmacopoeia*, or the persons who purchase it would object.

The solid opium is consumed exclusively by adults, men and women, but more by the latter than the former, in the proportion of 3 to 1.

The laudanum is partly consumed by adults, and to a considerable extent by infants. Godfrey's, or the Anodyne cordial, is almost exclusively consumed by infants. . . .

Among the poorest classes it is a common practice of mothers to administer Godfrey's cordial and laudanum to their infants; the object is to keep them quiet whilst the mother is at work. A case occurred a short time ago of a mother coming into the shop with her child in the arms. Witness remonstrated against giving it laudanum, and told the mother she had better go home and put the child in a bucket of water, "it would have been the most humane place of putting it out of the way." The mother replied that the infant had been used to the laudanum and must have it, and that it took a halfpenny worth a day, or 60 drops. Does not know what has become of the child, but "supposes it is done for by this time." It is not uncommon for mothers to begin this practice with infants of a fortnight old; commencing with half a teaspoonful of Godfrey's, or 1 or 2 drops of laudanum. Has known an infant killed with three drops of laudanum, but nothing was said about it. Knows that many infants die by degrees, and that no inquest or other inquiry is made. Has known some odd cases where surgeons have been called to apply the stomach pump; but "infants [die] quickly, they are not like grown people." A case of sudden death in an infant from laudanum occurred about three years ago, in which an inquest was held. . . . Heard that four children of the same family had died in the same way.

The Endless Day

For many working-class families, the boundaries between public work and private domestic life continually blurred. Although the industrial revolution transformed numerous jobs, workers continued to manufacture some goods, such as clothing, at home since they required no special equipment beyond a needle and thread or a sewing machine. In his 1856 study of the organization of work in different trades, French sociologist Adolphe-Jean Focillon described the household of a Parisian garment worker where work was very much a family affair. The "double day" experienced by the woman sounds strikingly familiar to what many women continue to experience today.

In the 1870s and 1880s, Mrs. Hugh Bell (Lady Bell), an upper-middle-class British writer and playwright, examined working-class life in a Yorkshire iron and steel-manufacturing town, conducting interviews with working-class families. The results of her investigations were published in her book, At the Works, *in which she discussed the different ways that working-class wives managed the family budget.*

F. G., who has 45 [shillings] a week, gives it all to his wife. She allows him 1 [shilling] a day pocket money, which he spends on sweets and chocolates. She also insists upon his paying 3 [pence] a day for his stout [beer] which she considers "a luxury and quite unnecessary." Another man . . . earns 50 [shillings] to 68 [shillings] a week. He gives his wife 28 [shillings] to keep house on, out of which he pays his sick club [a form of insurance society]. She appears to be a careful and thrifty woman and to do very well on it. What is done with the balance of her husband's wages is not stated. Another man, a laborer, who has 25 [shillings] a week, gives it all to his wife, and she gives him 2 [shillings] a week for pocket money. . . . Instances of this kind might be multiplied . . . where the woman has the upper hand, in spite of the wages being earned by the husband and her receiving them from him, she makes a favour of the amount she gives him back again.

The worker described in the present monograph lives in Paris. . . . He belongs to the large category of tailors and the conditions under which he works puts him in the group of workers known . . . as "piecers" [piece-rate workers]. With the worker lives a woman to whom he has taught the trade and who has become an indispensable aide to him in his profession. Thanks to the help she gives him, he is able to take on extra work on his own account, making suits for a clientele he has created for himself in the area around his home.

During his work the worker sits . . . on a large plank in front of the only window in the room where the family lives. He assembles the pre-cut pieces of the garments by hand, does the difficult needlework, and smoothes down the stitches with a hot iron. Other tasks, that require less strength and skill, are left for the

An entire family participates in making artificial flowers—even the four-year-old girl at the right, who separates the flower petals for her parents and brothers. At the turn of the twentieth century, families often worked long into the night in order to earn enough money to survive.

woman. In the summer, the worker labors eleven to twelve hours a day, and in winter, about ten hours a day. From the length of the workday one must deduct barely three quarters of an hour for the morning and midday meals. Every day he stops work at dinnertime, at five in the winter and at six or six thirty in the summer. He never works evenings, or Sundays and holidays.

[The woman] performs her principal tasks alongside the worker. She helps him make suits, whether for the employer's or the family's accounts. Seated on a chair near the plank where the worker sits, the woman constantly receives from him pieces of work he has prepared, along with instructions for completing them suitably. We estimate the wages of an assistant doing her work at three francs a day; but by doing piece work she raises her wages to four francs; on the other hand, she prolongs the workday long after the evening meal until eleven at night. In these conditions . . . she works 12 hours a day, 365 days a year. During these hours of labor, in addition to all the work done with the tailor, the woman does household tasks. She cleans the room, makes the beds, dresses the children, and prepares . . . the meals. Each week she washes the household linens, the children's clothes, and her dresses . . . at home in a glazed earthen bowl, then she goes down to the courtyard near the pump . . . to rinse them in two tubs loaned to her by a neighbor. She uses the free moments that the slackening of work in [the slow season] allows to mend the children's clothes, her linens, and those of the worker.

In 1843, Jemima Sanborn moved with her three daughters and son to the New England mill town of Nashua, New Hampshire, in search of work, leaving her husband and son to run their farm. In a letter to her friends, Richard and Ruth Bennett, she described the importance of each child's economic contribution to the family. Reliance on children's wages and income from boarders were as familiar to New England mill families as they were to English factory workers.

Y̲ou will probably want to know the cause of our moving here which are many. I will menshion a few of them. One of them is the hard times to get a living off the farm for so large a family so we have devided our family for this year. We have left Plummer and Luther to care for the farm and granmarm and Aunt Polly. The rest of us have moved to Nashvill [a part of Nashua] thinking the girls and Charles they would probely work in the Mill. But we have had bad luck in giting them in only Jane has got in yet. Ann has the promis of going to the mill next week. Hannah is going to school. We are in hopes to take a few boarders but have not got any yet.

Frederich Engels, co-author with Karl Marx of the *Communist Manifesto*, a 1848 call to worker revolution, sympathized with the plight of industrial workers. In the early 1840s, Engels traveled to England on business and published his observations on the rampant poverty and overcrowded conditions in which English workers lived. In his 1845 book, *The Condition of the Working Class in England*, Engels blamed women's wage earning on the fact that men's low wages could not support a family. He believed that the employment of women in factories had a terrible influence on domestic life because it left women little time to spend with their families.

The employment of the wife dissolves the family utterly and of necessity, and this dissolution in our present society, which is based upon the family, brings the most demoralizing consequences for parents as well as children. A mother who has no time to trouble herself about her child, to perform the most ordinary, loving services for it during its first year, who scarcely indeed sees it, can be no real mother to the child, must inevitably grow indifferent to it, treat it unlovingly like a stranger. The children who grow up under such conditions are utterly ruined for later family life, can never feel at home in the family which they themselves found, because they have been accustomed to isolation and contribute therefore to the already general undermining of the family in the working class. . . .

In many cases, the family is not wholly dissolved by the employment of the wife, but turned upside down. The wife supports the family, the husband sits at home, tends the children, sweeps the room and cooks. This case happens very frequently; in Manchester alone, many hundred such men could be cited, condemned to domestic occupations. It is easy to imagine the wrath aroused among the workingmen by this reversal of all relations within the family while the other social conditions remain unchanged. . . .

Can anyone imagine a more insane state of things . . . ? Yet, this condition, which unsexes the man and takes from the woman all womanliness . . . this condition which degrades in the most shameful way both sexes, and through them, Humanity, is the last result of our much praised civilization, the final achievement of all the efforts and struggles of hundreds of generations to improve their own situation and that of their posterity. We must . . . that so total a reversal of the position of the sexes can have come to pass only

A STORY OF A SEWING MACHINE OPERATOR.
Bertha, the Sewing-Machine Girl;

"If you will listen to my love, Miss Bascomb, you shall ride in your carriage!"

OR,
DEATH AT THE WHEEL!
By FRANCIS S. SMITH,
Author of "Alice Blake," "Maggie the Charity Child," "Eveleen Wilson," etc.

"Bertha, the Sewing-Machine Girl," a popular serialized story appearing in the New York Weekly *newspaper, followed the travails of a sweatshop worker in the 1870s. In this issue, Bertha is propositioned by a well-dressed man who promises her a ride in a carriage if she will only return his affections. Sexual harassment of working-class women on the job was not uncommon during the industrial revolution.*

because the sexes have been placed in a false position from the beginning. If the reign of the wife over the husband, as inevitably brought about by the factory system, is inhuman, the pristine rule of the husband over the wife must have been inhuman, too. . . .

The unmarried women who have grown up in the mills are no better off than the married ones. It is self-evident that a girl who has worked in a mill from her ninth year is in no position to understand domestic work, whence it follows that female operatives prove wholly inexperienced and unfit as housekeepers. They cannot knit or sew, cook or wash, and are unacquainted with the most ordinary duties of a housekeeper, and when they have young children, they have not the vaguest idea how to set about it.

Chapter Five

Global Repercussions

The industrial revolution that began in England and spread to the United States and continental Europe by the 1840s and 1850s had tremendous effects around the world. Although England, western Europe, and the United States were the first major areas to experience industrial revolutions, by the end of the nineteenth century, other countries—notably Russia, Japan, and Sweden, among others—joined in. Even parts of the world that did not industrialize were touched by the power of new inventions, machines, and manufacturing processes and by the products that the wheels of industry churned out. For the captains of industry produced goods in order to sell, trade, or barter them, and their commercial activities circled the globe.

The slave trade provided labor for the cotton plantations of the United States, which in turn fueled the cotton textile industry and the industrial revolution in England, illustrates this global trading network. Slaves from Africa were transported not only to the United States, they were also shipped to the Caribbean, where the French and the British grew sugar and manufactured rum. The slave trade began in the 1500s when the Portuguese and Spanish began shipping human cargo to Brazil and South America. In the 1700s, it expanded astronomically once other Europeans—the French, British and Dutch, for example—realized how profitable it could be to trade in slaves who could be used as free labor growing cotton, tobacco, and coffee and producing sugar. Although historians disagree about the extent to which the slave trade provided the money (capital) to invest in industry, most acknowledge that the industrial revolution in British cotton textiles was intimately linked to the enslavement of African men and women.

The industrial revolution also made it necessary for manufacturers to have access to a continuous supply of raw materials and markets in

British clipper ships unload cargo in the British-controlled port of Calcutta, India. Trade with colonial markets made up a significant portion of British overseas commerce, particularly for the purchase of raw materials and sale of British manufactured goods.

New Orleans businessmen inspect cotton in 1873 before shipping bales of it to Europe and elsewhere in the United States. Cotton from the southern United States helped to feed both the American and European textile industries through the nineteenth century.

which to sell manufactured goods. One way to do this was by building overseas empires in undeveloped parts of the world that were rich in natural resources, a policy called imperialism. The British North American and Caribbean colonies, sources of tobacco and cotton, were one example; France's colonies in Indochina, sources of silk, were another. Imperial domination was key to extracting resources—whether rubber in the Congo conquered by Belgium at the end of the nineteenth century or diamonds and tin in South African mines controlled by the Dutch and British. Industrialization and the ability to harness steam to boats and build better weapons helped Europeans and Americans secure control of these areas and dominate the globe economically and politically by the end of the nineteenth century. These areas of the world also kept the machinery of industrialization turning, for they provided the markets where British, French, or Belgian manufacturers could sell their manufactured goods. Some of these goods (cheap consumer goods such as cotton cloth) benefited colonized peoples. But until Britain banned slavery in its colonies in 1833 and the French did the same in 1848, many colonial subjects worked as slaves or forced laborers or under harsh conditions at very low wages.

Finally, by the end of the nineteenth century, other countries joined the roster of those that had experienced industrial revolutions, Russia and Japan foremost among them. Russia's industrial revolution occurred more slowly than that of Britain. While Britain and the United States were industrializing, Russia remained a predominantly agricultural society that relied on the West for imported manufactured goods. Serfdom thrived in the Russian countryside and peasants who were not serfs eked out an existence on their farms. But the winds of change were blowing. Two things happened in the second half of the nineteenth century: The emancipation of Russian serfs in 1861 meant that large numbers of rural folk were now free to work in large cities. Second, massive railway building in the 1870s allowed Russia to exploit its immense natural resources of coal and iron more effectively than ever before, and factories began to appear in cities such as Moscow and St. Petersburg. Like workers in the West, Russian workers labored long hours for very low wages, often sleeping on their benches in workshops or factories. In some factories, employers treated workers like serfs, paying them only twice a year, and everywhere employers imposed the same discipline as western European and American employers. Working-class unrest exploded in the Revolution of 1905, when workers protested low wages and poor working conditions in Russian factories, and again in the famous Bolshevik Revolution of 1917, when workers protested harsh factory conditions and deprivation during World War I.

Japan also industrialized around the same time as Russia, beginning in the 1860s and 1870s. Like Russia, Japan benefited from the support of the government in building railroads, crucial to transporting natural resources and creating a national market for manufactured goods. The Japanese government also abolished guilds, liberating workers and allowing industrial innovation to occur freely—just as in the early stages of industrialization in the West. The government took a major role in supporting and operating metalworking factories, shipyards, and mines, and a vibrant silk industry emerged. Much as in the West, women's low wages in factories and in home-based textile manufacture (domestic industry) enabled the silk industry to profit by lowering production costs. Some women even worked as indentured servants. Like Western industrial powers, Japan attempted to establish colonies in nearby China and Korea as a way to insure a supply of raw materials and markets in the 1890s. Although no country industrialized

Sweden's industrial revolution, like Japan's and Russia's, occurred late in the nineteenth century. In an interview conducted in the 1950s, Carl Lund, a Swedish metalworker, reflected on the state of his trade in the 1880s. His comments show how, even in the midst of industrialization, not all industries had mechanized.

Tools and methods of working were relatively primitive. The lathes were constructed from iron-plated wood. To turn them meant revolving a large balance wheel. This was generally the job of the apprentice and an extremely arduous and little loved task it was. For exceptionally heavy jobs, they would sometimes hire a pauper from the workhouse to do the donkeywork. The only method available for cutting threads was by hand. Drilling was accomplished using tools similar to those with which the [people] of the Congo made their fires. Wedges were formed by hand, the necessary machines being unknown in this workshop.

in precisely the same way as any other, strikingly similar patterns linked industrial revolutions all over the globe.

World Trade in Slaves

From roughly 1500 to 1865, a lucrative slave trade supported by the major governments of the world provided free labor for the sugar plantations of the Caribbean and the tobacco and cotton plantations of the American South. Indeed, the Europeans made the trade in human cargo and the use of slavery a global phenomenon, as shown by this 1752 article by French writer Le Romain on the slave trade from West Africa to the West Indies. Le Romain's article appeared in France as an entry in a multivolume catalogue of information called the *Encyclopedia.* The men who compiled the *Encyclopedia,* French writers Jean d'Alembert and Denis Diderot, wanted to make their readers aware of the slave trade and slave labor.

For the last few centuries the Europeans have carried on a trade in Negroes whom they obtain from Guinea and other coasts of Africa and whom they use to maintain the colonies established in various parts of America and in the West Indies. To justify this loathsome commerce, which is contrary to natural law, it is argued that ordinarily these slaves find the salvation of their souls in the loss of their liberty, and that the Christian teaching they receive, together with their indispensable role in the cultivation of sugar cane, tobacco, indigo, etc., softens the apparent inhumanity of a commerce where men buy and sell their fellow men as they would animals used in the cultivation of the land.

Trade in Negroes is carried on by all the nations that have settlements in the West Indies, and especially by the French, the English, the Portuguese, the Dutch, the Swedes, and the Danes . . . . The best Negroes are obtained from Cape Verde, Angola, Senegal, the kingdom of the Jaloffes, the kingdom of Galland, from Damel, from the river Gambia, Majugard, Bar, etc.

These slaves are procured in various ways. Some, to escape famine and destitution, sell themselves, their children, and wives to the kings and the most powerful men among them, who have the means to feed them: for even though the Negroes in general have very modest needs, certain parts of Africa are at times so extraordinarily barren, particularly when, as is common, a cloud of locusts

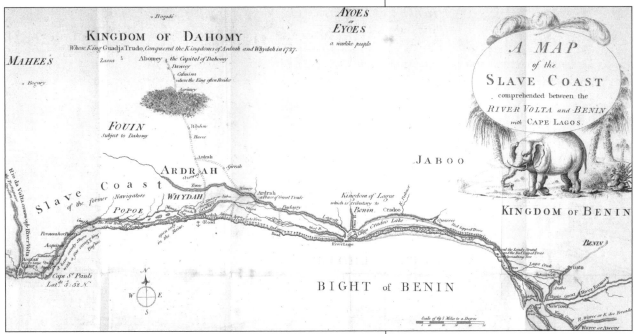

As this 1789 map indicates, this section of the West African coast near the Volta River, Benin, and Cape Lagos was an important center for the slave trade before the industrial revolution. The French and English brought African slaves to Europe and the Americas, including the Caribbean islands, where they performed agricultural labor and also worked as domestic servants.

has passed through, that no crop of millet or rice can be harvested, nor any other vegetable that is their customary diet. Others are prisoners taken during wars or in the course of the raids these minor kings carry out on neighboring lands, often with no other object than to get slaves whom they bring back with them: the young, the old, women, girls, even babies at their mothers' breast.

As soon as the trade is completed no time must be lost in setting sail. Experience has shown that as long as these unfortunates are still within sight of their homeland they are overcome by sorrow and gripped by despair. The former is the cause of many illnesses from which a large number perish during the crossing; the latter inclines them to suicide, which they effect either by refusing nourishment or by shutting off their breathing. This they do in a way they know of turning and twisting their tongues which unfailingly suffocates them. Others again shatter their head against the sides of the ship or throw themselves into the sea if the occasion presents itself . . .

When they arrive in the West Indies they are sold for three to five hundred livres, according to their age, their strength, and their health. Ordinarily they are not paid for in cash but in local products.

Negroes constitute the principal wealth of the inhabitants of the West Indies. Anyone who owns a dozen can be considered rich. Since they multiply a great deal in hot countries, their

Two European slave traders beat an African man as a woman and her child are led away by another slave trader. The slave trade separated hundreds of thousands of African men and women from their families and took them far from home to labor on the plantations of the Caribbean and the American South.

masters, provided they treat them kindly, can witness a steady increase in families who are born into slavery. Their robust nature demands that they should be treated neither with excessive indulgence nor with excessive harshness. Moderate punishment renders them obedient and stimulates them to work, but excessive strictness makes them sullen and drives them to join the *nègres marons*, or wild Negroes, who inhabit inaccessible regions of these islands, where they would rather put up with a most wretched life than return to slavery.

The Negroes' work on the Plantations. For the cultivation of sugar cane, coffee, cocoa, manioc, cotton, indigo, and annato the number of slaves needed is in proportion to the size of the plantation. Several slaves are taught the type of work required to cultivate these products well. All of them are under the orders of a white or black overseer who in his turn is subordinate to a manager on the large plantations.

The Negroes who are assigned to the principal operations in the sugar refineries are called refiners *(raffineurs).* It is not easy for them to acquire a perfect command of their art. This requires an apprenticeship of several years during which they have to work very diligently. Their work is all the more tiring because they are continually exposed to the heat of the cauldrons in which sugar is made. The carpenters and pit-sawyers are responsible for repairing the mill and, together with the masons, for the upkeep of the various buildings of the refinery. Cartwrights are very essential, it is hardly possible to get along without coopers and in the large establishments a smith finds much work to do. All the other slaves, with the exception of the domestic servants, are employed every day in cultivating the land, looking after the plantings, harrowing the savannahs and pastures, and cutting the sugar cane, which is transported to the mill by carters and mule-drivers. In the mill we commonly find Negro women whose task it is to pass the cane through rollers, large metal cylinders, which press out the juice from which sugar is made. Those Negroes who have the poorest physique and are the least suited to difficult work are detailed to the maintenance of the fires in the furnace of the sugar mill and the evaporator; they look after the sick in the infirmary or guard the cattle on the savannahs. The little negro boys and girls are also set to tasks that are in proportion to their strength. Thus on every plantation the masters and managers must put as much effort as possible into studying the character, strength, dispositions, and talents of the slaves, so that they may put them to good use.

British and French reformers fought hard to end the European commerce in African slaves and in 1807 the British Parliament voted to abolish the slave trade. Scottish economist Charles Mackenzie praised this action, but in his 1811 pamphlet, *Facts Relative to the Present State of the British Cotton Colonies*, he also argued that Parliament should support planters who depended on slaves. Eventually Britain abolished slavery in its colonies in 1833.

As a man, I rejoice at the abolition of the slave trade, and I regard the day in which the final seal was given to that great act of deliberative wisdom and justice as the brightest in the records of humanity; but while I would cherish every generous feeling in behalf of much wronged Africa, there is no necessity for banishing every sentiment of justice towards our own country-men. Bad as the slave trade undoubtedly was, it was sanctioned by successive Monarchs, Ministers, and Parliaments.—Encouraged by this sanction, colonists settled and cultivated lands, and devoted their whole resources to them: Many of the speculators were young and unreflecting men, who by chance had been thrown into this active scene, and without entering into an examination of the merits or demerits of the transactions, engaged in what received the approbation of their country. Justice has recently been rendered, in a pre-eminent degree, to the nations of Africa, let it now be rendered to British subjects, whose errors were sanctioned and promoted by the mother country. The colonists only ask for a just and fair protection . . . The voice of Parliament, it is to be hoped, will confirm their claims.

Empire Building

The industrial revolution had a tremendous impact on parts of the world that had not yet industrialized. Although Europeans had traded for centuries with parts of Asia, India, the Caribbean islands and Hawaii, industrialization stimulated the establishment of colonies to ensure a steady supply of raw materials, such as cotton. Scottish economist Charles Mackenzie discussed the importance of the British and other colonies for cotton manufacture in his pamphlet, *Facts Relative to the Present State of the British Cotton Colonies*, published in 1811.

The demand for British produce, the want of which cannot be dispensed with, is so enormous as to call forth directly and indirectly the energies of every part of the empire. An immense number of men are employed by the manufacturers, who are thus supported: British merchants, ship owners, insurance brokers, and others, are actually maintained by the West India colonies; and from the same source is derived above one-third of the whole of the cotton imported into Great Britain. . . .

Raw cotton has become, nearly, with wool, a staple of these kingdoms. The unrivaled excellence of our manufactures ensures us the market wherever we have access. At present we derive the cotton . . . which is manufactured or exported in its raw state, from our own colonies, from the United States of America, the Brazils, the Spanish colonies, the Levant, and the East Indies. Of the whole of this, above one-third is imported from the British colonies. On this we can always calculate, baring the risk of crops, and of capture; the last being much lessened by the expulsion of the French from the western hemisphere. All obtained from foreigners is

African-American workers pick cotton and load cotton bales for transport to Europe and distant parts of the United States on this 1880 advertisement for thread. The fact that all the cotton workers are black illustrates the continued racial division of labor in cotton production after the end of slavery.

Levant

Modern Israel, Jordan, Lebanon, and the Palestinian territories dependent on their caprice; of this America has recently afforded an admirable illustration.

In 1808, the quantity of cotton imported from North America was only *ten millions and a half lbs.* being thus reduced to little more than one third of what it had been for the three preceding years. . . . There are also physical objections to some of the cotton . . . obtained from foreign sources: that from the Levant being only fit for the coarsest manufactures; and that from India being either course or fine in the extreme, cannot be generally used. The expense, too, of freight is four times greater than that from the West Indies. . . .

From the very nature of our West India colonies, they are even now, and must be at all periods, in a great measure dependent on other countries for some of the most important necessaries of life. The constitution of the society precludes manufacturing the most common articles, and they possess few of the means of support.

As industrialism progressed, European countries sought even greater control over raw materials and resources to feed the industrial machine. Expanding European empires and overseas colonies provided those resources and control. Otto von Bismarck, German Chancellor in the 1870s and 1880s, reviewed the importance of colonies for Europe and Germany in speeches to the German Reichstag (parliament) in 1885.

March 1885

If the British value their colonies there so highly, if they . . . hold the positions they have gained there with such commendable energy—is all this . . . a mere whim? Are there not likely to be concrete British interests behind this, the hope to sell by means of the coastal trading posts British manufactures in large masses into the interior of Africa, to the hundreds of millions of people living in these countries, who are gradually becoming used to an increased consumption of European goods? . . .

I think the most promising colonies are those of New Guinea. . . . According to my information, there are large and easily cultivable territories . . . on the equator, which are therefore . . . suitable for the cultivation of coffee, cotton and similar tropical products. . . .

Colonies like Cuba, like Puerto Rico, like the West Indies and the equatorial colonies are always given a high monetary value by their mother country. The main thing is to set up plantations there

Vladimir Ilyich Lenin, a leader of the Russian Revolution of 1917, believed that industrial revolutions were destined to lead to imperialism because to keep up profits, manufacturers would have to invest abroad. He discussed how European powers used their money (capital) in his 1905 book Imperialism: the Highest Stage of Capitalism.

The principal spheres of investment of British capital are the British colonies, which are very large . . . in America (for example, Canada), not to mention Asia, etc. In this case, enormous exports of capital are bound up most closely with vast colonies. . . . In the case of France the situation is different. French capital exports are invested mainly in Europe, primarily in Russia (at least 10 billion francs). This is mainly *loan* capital, government loans, and not capital invested in industrial undertakings. . . . In the case of Germany, we have a third type: colonies are [not that important] and German capital invested abroad is divided most evenly between Europe and America.

and to employ Germans with the highest or an advanced education on these plantations. . . . Let us assume that a part of the coffee or the cotton that we import, is grown on German soil overseas, would this not represent an increase in the German national wealth?

At present we buy all our cotton from America and are dependent on the American monopoly. . . . If we were to plant and cultivate cotton with the same intelligence as the Americans, in districts like New Guinea, the Cameroon, the African equatorial districts which grow cotton, we would then not buy from the foreigner but from German overseas planters. This would be an advantage for our national income, while at present the money we are spending on cotton, coffee, copra [the kernel of the cocoa nut used for cocoa-nut oil] and all other similar equatorial products are a total loss for our national wealth.

Over the course of the nineteenth century, European countries extended the reach of their empires in Africa and Southeast Asia. Jules Ferry, who twice served as prime minister of France published these views on imperialism in 1890 in a book on French colonization of Indochina—an area especially valued for its raw silk. His observations show how nineteenth-century statesmen linked empire to industrial development and also to social peace.

Colonial policy is a daughter of industrial policy. For rich nations, where capital is abundant and accumulates rapidly, where manufactures constantly increase, exportation is an essential factor of public prosperity, and the field for the investment of capital, as the demand for labor, is measured by the extent of the foreign market. If it had been possible to establish among manufacturing nations something like the industrial division of labour, a methodical and rational division of industries according to aptitudes and the natural and social economic conditions of the different producing nations, placing the cotton industry here, metallurgy there, reserving for one sugar and spirits, for another silk and wool, perhaps Europe would not have had to search outside its own boundaries for markets for its wares. . . . But today the whole world wants to spin and weave, to forge and distill. All Europe is making sugar as fast as it can, and is trying to export it. . . .

The plethora of capital in industry does not tend merely to diminish profits, but it also halts the increase in wages, which is

Nineteenth-century French economist Paul Leroy Beaulieu believed that European imperial powers had a moral obligation to provide colonized people with the benefits of industrial civilization. Beaulieu harbored racist assumptions about the inferiority of colonized groups and supported an idea common among advocates of imperialism, the notion that Europeans had a "civilizing mission" to accomplish.

The present-day world is composed of . . . different . . . types of civilization. . . . In the [one] part live peoples . . . which either stagnated or had not been able to constitute themselves as unified, peaceful, progressive nations. . . . a great part of the world is inhabited by barbarian tribes or savages, some given over to wars without end and to brutal customs, and others knowing so little of the arts and being so little accustomed to work and invention that they do not know how to exploit their land and its natural riches. This state of the world implies for the civilized peoples a right of intervention . . . in the affairs of the peoples of [these] categories. . . .

Imperialism entails a profound action on a people and a territory, providing the inhabitants with some education and regular justice, teaching them the division of labor and the uses of capital when they are ignorant of these things. It opens an area not only to the merchandise of the mother country, but to its capital and its savings, to its engineers, its overseers, to its emigrants. . . . Such a transformation of a barbarian country cannot be accomplished by simple commercial relations.

the natural and beneficent law of modern societies. And this is not just an abstract law, but a phenomenon of flesh and bone, of passion and the will, which agitates, complains, and protects itself. Social peace is, in the industrial age of humanity, a question of markets. . . . The European market is saturated; it is necessary to discover new groups of consumers in other parts of the world, or to put modern society in bankruptcy and to prepare for a cataclysmic social liquidation in the dawn of the twentieth century, the consequences of which are impossible to foretell.

The American pavilion at London's Great Exhibition of 1851 showcased American inventions, including the McCormick grain harvester, the Colt revolver, and Goodyear's vulcanized rubber, the raw material for which had been imported from the Congo in Africa. Americans hoped to interest Europeans in the products of their industrial revolution.

Global Industrialization

By the late nineteenth century, industrialization had spread well beyond western Europe. Russia, for example, benefited from the earlier industrialization of other European countries and relied heavily on the West for money and technical expertise for everything from railway building to textile machinery. In 1900, Henry Cooke, a British diplomatic official, wrote this report on the trans-Siberian railway which, begun in 1892 and finished in 1916, linked Moscow with the eastern port of Vladivostock on the Sea of Japan. Railways

enabled Russia to expand its control over the Russian Empire and were crucial to the development of a national market. Cooke marveled at the vast distances linked by rail.

It is indeed not too much to say that the completion of this gigantic thoroughfare, which is to bring Paris into direct overland communication with Vladivostock, will, commercially and otherwise, be one of the greatest events of the opening years of the new century. . . .

Dealing with a vast expanse of territory exceeding in area the whole of Europe, and some 40 times the size of the British Isles, it would require a volume . . . to give any adequate idea of the diversities of the country and climate, its peoples and customs, its old and new land routes and immeasurable waterways, or, in general, to describe the resources and possibilities included in the term Siberia. What it is, and at the same time what it might be, even when duly considering its extensive Polar wastes, is seen from the fact that the total population of this greater Russia has but lately begun to exceed that of London. [The railroad] will be to Russia's increasing millions what British dependencies have been to the United Kingdom. The railroad now approaching completion will

A Russian train carries passengers and goods into the countryside, while a group of peasants, some children, and a priest have come to watch this symbol of industrialization pass by their town. In the nineteenth century, Russia, with the help of French investors, began building railroads across its immense territory, linking the countryside to urban industrial centers.

Men produce tools in a Swedish forge around the end of the nineteenth century. Even after industrialization led to the creation of huge machines for producing iron and steel, small workshops like this one continued to flourish.

give the desired impetus to colonization and development, and by making the whole country a vast transit route between east and west open it out to the whole world.

Moscow was a bustling center of industrial activity by the end of the nineteenth century. Russian metalworker Semon I. Kanatchikov described his apprenticeship in the pattern shop of a Moscow engineering company in 1895 in his 1929 autobiography, *The Story of My Life*. Pattern workers made the forms used to craft the metal parts for steam engines, pumps, and scales. Kanatchikov noted the relatively primitive state of tools and working conditions. Like workers in other parts of the world, he put in long hours.

In those days, patternmakers still worked with their own tools. A good patternmaker, when he started work at a new factory, was expected to bring a case of tools along, and some factories even required that he have his own workbench. My first act was to begin to fashion myself a joiner plane and a chisel out of strong beechwood. At first my tools were not completely satisfactory, but they were good enough to use. My hands were still poorly trained; they lacked the dexterity and strength to cut hard wood with care and precision.

I also learned how to use a turning lathe. The work absorbed me greatly since I soon learned to carve all kinds of wooden knick-knacks—wine-glasses, little tumblers, eggs, pencilcases, and so on. True, sometimes my excessive love for knickknacks cost me a

E. A. Oliunina, a social researcher, described this scene in a garment-making workshop in Moscow in 1910–1911. It suggests that garment manufacturers all over the world experienced similar conditions.

I encountered one shop where work was carried on in a kitchen that had one window and only 0.8 cubic meters [about 2 cubic feet per person]. Here they heat the flat irons [used for pressing the fabric], here they keep the bucket with food garbage, and here they cook. Fumes and smoke fill the room. But if the window vent is opened, there is a draft. The shop also serves as an eating and sleeping place for workers. There are no mattresses and the workers sleep on wood benches, covering themselves with whatever they can find. One such shop makes dresses for a certain large capitalist firm; another makes men's suits for the public market.

whack across the head from the foreman, but that didn't bother me very much. . . .

In general, our lives were peaceful and harmonious, a small paradise. Only one thing was wrong—our workday was too long: eleven and a half hours. But even that problem was soon removed without a struggle. After the St. Petersburg weavers' strike of 1896, our sagacious employer . . . immediately introduced the ten-hour day at his factory. After than, our group of skilled workers began to live as well as could be.

By about 1870, Japan also began to experience an industrial revolution. As in Europe and the United States, textile manufacturing led Japan's industrial development. Japanese silk came to be known all over the world for its high quality. In the 1880s, a German professor of geography, J. J. Rein, traveled to Japan and published a book in 1889 describing the progress of the Japanese luxury industries. He discussed how Japanese manufacturers faced stiff competition from silk fabric already being produced for the world market by Britain and France. Rein believed that the success of the Japanese silk industry depended on its ability to mechanize, use cheap labor, and compete in the international market.

When, at the Vienna Exhibition of 1873, Japan for the first time displayed the variety, richness, and tasteful collection of its . . . silk factories, not only were the ordinary visitors astonished at these unsuspected accomplishments, but even more, the well-informed Prize Commissioners. There were simple, smooth stuffs, and surprisingly beautiful twilled fabrics full of softness and elegance, with heavy brocades and other figured materials of a beauty utterly unanticipated, besides some entirely new appliances and designs. Though it is true the Chinese were the teachers and models to the Japanese in silk manufactures, yet here, as in so many other instances, the pupil has outstripped the master. . . .

While the silk culture of Japan received a great impulse at the opening of the new commerce . . . silk manufacture has been much and variously damaged thereby. The cheap cotton and wool stuffs thrown upon the market from foreign countries for several decades, compete constantly more strongly with silk materials. Most of the velvet looms were obliged a few years ago to suspend competition with the extraordinarily cheap cotton velvets of Manchester. And it has come about that the export of raw silk,

Japanese women sort and wash cocoons and spin silk thread, tasks usually considered "women's work." Silk production was as important to Japanese industrial development as cotton textiles were to Britain's industrial revolution.

beginning in 1859 and rapidly increasing in succeeding years, to which that of silkworm eggs was soon added, has had a great influence on the price of raw silk, which has risen in a few years . . . ten or sixteen fold. Many of the Japanese, under such circumstances, found themselves obliged to give up their custom of wearing silk clothing, and to use the much cheaper [wool] and cotton material.

[The] Japanese silk industry on the other hand, with all its fine products, could not gain new markets of any consequence, for the change from hand to machine weaving has not yet taken place with them. . . . After the steam loom had begun to revolutionize the silk industry in Europe, there could be no more Japanese competition. Not until the example of Europe in this respect is followed will the cheaper labour power and greater skill and aptitude avail to put the Japanese on a new basis of competition with foreign countries in its silk industry. And that of course opens to [home-based] industry no very inviting future. As the [mill] founded at Tomioka in 1872 with its steam power rendered the small reeling establishments, which could no longer compete with it, gradually useless, hundreds of web looms and those dependent upon them will be concerned in the new manner of silk manufacture.

Chapter Six

Protest and Resistance

On a crisp fall day in October 1836, a textile factory work-er in Lowell, Massachusetts, stood by the window of the workshop looking down into the courtyard below. When one of her sister workers tossed her hat in the air, she and the rest of the women in the workshop quietly filed out of the work-shop into the factory yard and declared themselves on strike against a wage cut. Soon, somewhere between 1,550 and 2,000 workers had joined them, shutting down many of the large textile mills in Massachusetts' Merrimack River valley and leading to the formation of the Factory Girls' Association. To proclaim their rights to better con-ditions as free working women, and to contrast their freedom with the bondage of their African-American sisters laboring on the plantations of the American South, they marched in front of the factories, singing,

> "Oh isn't it a pity, such a pretty girl as I—
> Should be sent into the factory to pine away and die?
> Oh I cannot be a slave,
> I will not be a slave,
> For I'm so fond of liberty,
> That I cannot be a slave."

This women's protest was not the first strike of its kind in the United States, nor in the industrialized world. Women had already gone on strike in Pawtucket in 1824 and the first strike in Lowell occurred in 1834; but the 1836 strike symbolized how workers reacted to indus-trial conditions in the nineteenth century and later. Far from being the passive and compliant workers that employers hoped they would be, these young women challenged their employers.

As industrialization swept through Europe, the United States, and elsewhere, workers became increasingly resentful of how manufactur-ers profited from their hard work and the growing social inequalities

The images on this 1877 print repre-sent the values of the Brotherhood of Locomotive Engineers of the United States and Canada: justice, sobriety, morality, protection of workers and truth. Trade unions in Europe and North America used emblems such as this to establish a sense of identity and tradition.

between themselves and their employers. Some of the very earliest forms of worker protest, in the beginning of the nineteenth century, targeted machines. Many men and women feared that new technologies, the hallmark of the industrial revolution, promised not progress and prosperity, but a loss of skill, status, wages, and employment. But, as many discovered, protests against machines could not stop the inexorable march of technological development that started at the beginning of the nineteenth century. Gradually workers came to accept the fact that machines were there to stay, and turned their attention to efforts to reform the low pay, long hours, and dreadfully unsafe conditions in which they worked.

From the very beginning of the industrial revolution, workers organized in labor unions to defend their interests and used strikes to pressure employers to improve basic conditions of work and wages. The workers' concerns were part of larger "quality of life" issues that are surprisingly similar to what working people all over the world face today. Nineteenth-century workers sought respect for their skills and abilities on the job, a decent and honorable standard of living, and the right to leisure for recreation and time with their families. But both states and employers vigorously resisted workers' efforts to take collective action. On both sides of the Atlantic, governments supported employers' efforts to repress labor organization. France, Britain, and Germany all made workers' organizations of any kind illegal until the end of the nineteenth century. In the United States and Europe, employers combated unions by firing or locking workers out of the factory and freely used police force to repress workers' peaceful demonstrations. Some workers avoided repression by forming mutual aid or friendly societies—organizations that were designed to provide support to workers and their families at times of illness or during periods of unemployment. Others formed producers' and consumers' cooperatives to enable workers to benefit directly from their labor and to buy goods more cheaply.

Socialist thinkers in France, Britain, and Germany also criticized the social and economic inequalities of industrial capitalism. Socialism was the philosophy that in order for workers—not just the middle class—to benefit from the industrial revolution, major social and economic changes had to occur. Some proposed establishing communities in which workers would control production instead of factory owners and enjoy the profits of their labors. German thinkers Karl Marx and Frederick Engels, however, believed that industrial capitalism was destined to exploit workers

A poster in both English and German summons Chicago workers—including the city's sizable German working class—to a meeting in 1886 in Haymarket Square. At the meeting, called to protest the fatal shooting by police of workers who had peacefully demonstrated for the eight-hour day, a bomb killed a police officer and shots fired by police injured numerous bystanders.

Women workers and wives appeal to their striking male coworkers and husbands not to return to their jobs at the Le Creusot coal mines in France in 1870. At this demonstration, about 3,000 workers struck for higher wages and shorter hours.

by driving down their wages and getting them to work longer hours in order for middle-class capitalists to profit. This meant an inevitable conflict of interest between the bourgeoisie (employers) and the proletariat (workers). According to Marx and Engels, for real change to occur, the proletariat had to overthrow the bourgeoisie by means of a violent revolution. A more just socialist society would then rise from the ashes of the old capitalist order. The ideas of Marx and Engels had a powerful influence on the labor movement and eventually became the ideological force behind communist political parties that emphasized the revolutionary aspects of socialism worldwide.

Throughout the history of protest and resistance, gender and racial differences dramatically influenced labor movements, much as they shaped industrial labor. Although unions claimed to stand for improving all workers' lives, labor and socialist activists addressed their appeals mainly to white males. In the United States, unions often openly opposed admitting African-American and foreign workers. Unions systematically excluded women from their ranks, arguing that because women earned less than men, they would hurt men's efforts to secure higher wages. Some labor activists supported a family wage so that wives and children would not have to work. But despite these obstacles, women and African Americans in the United States participated in labor protest. In the first decade of the twentieth century, women formed their own unions, such as the women's Trade Union League, established in the United States in 1903. Overall, workers' resistance to oppressive and exploitative conditions was one of the positive outcomes of the industrial revolution. Many workers' protests bore fruit, and eventually governments in both Europe and United States passed laws to reduce working hours and outlaw child labor.

From Violence to Organization

In 1811 and 1812, French and English textile workers violently protested against shearing machines that cut the fuzz (nap) from the surface of woolen cloth. These machines displaced skilled men who formerly used huge shears to perform this operation manually. In England, workers sent warning letters to employers, signed "Ned Ludd," demanding that they cease to use the machines and threatening violence if they did not. Ned Ludd probably never existed, but protesters used his name so regularly that machine breakers became known as "Luddites." In Huddersfield, England, a group of workers sent this warning of violence to a textile manufacturer in 1812.

SIR,

Information has just been given in, that you are a holder of those detestable Shearing Frames, and I was desired by my men to write to you, and give you fair warning to pull them down, and . . . if they are not taken down by the end of next week, I shall detach one of my lieutenants with at least 300 men to destroy them, and further more take notice that . . . we will increase your misfortunes by burning your buildings down to ashes, and if you have the impudence to fire at any of my men, they have orders to murder you and burn all your Housing. You will have the goodness to go to your neighbours to inform them that the same Fate awaits them if their Frames are not taken down, as I understand there are several in your neighbourhood. . . . we will never lay down our arms till the House of Commons passes an act to put down all the machinery hurtfull to the Commonality and repeal that to the Frame Breakers—but we petition no more, that wont do, fighting must.

Signed by the General of the Army of Redressers
NED LUDD
Clerk.

Protection

FOR THE
INDUSTRIOUS
Weavers.

INFORMATION having been received that a great number of industrious Weavers have been deterred by threats and acts of violence from the pursuit of their lawful occupations, and that in many instances their Shuttles have been taken, and their Materials damaged by persons acting under the existing Combinations :

Notice is hereby Given,

That every Protection will be afforded to persons so injured, upon giving Information to the Constables of Stockport: And a Reward of

FIFTY GUINEAS

Will be paid, on conviction, to the person who will come forward with such evidence as may be the means of convicting any one or more of the offences mentioned in the Act of Parliament, of which an Extract is subjoined : And a Reward of

TWENTY GUINEAS

Will be paid, on conviction, to the person who will come forward and inform of any person being guilty of assaulting or molesting industrious and honest Weavers, so as to prevent them from taking out or bringing in their Work peaceably.

Stockport, June 17th, 1808.　　　PETER BROWN,
　　　　　　　　　　　　　T. CARTWRIGHT, } CONSTABLES.

By the 22nd, Geo. 3, C. 40, S. 3.

It is enacted, " That if any person enter, by force, into any House or Shop, with intent to Cut and Destroy any Linen or Cotton, or Linen and Cotton mixed with any other Materials, in the Loom, or any Warp or Shute, Tools, Tackle, and Utensils, or shall Cut or Destroy the same, or shall Break and Destroy any Tools, Tackle, or Utensils, for Weaving, Preparing, or Making any such Manufactures, every such Offender shall be guilty of FELONY, without Benefit of Clergy".

This 1808 poster promises that the industrial city of Stockport, England, will protect weavers using new mechanized looms from violence by the handloom weavers who were displaced by the new machines.

In the early 1800s, some reformers believed that workers could avoid the hardships of industrial work by organizing producers' cooperatives where they managed production collectively (instead of working for employers) and reaped the profits. British newspaper editor George Mudie published this appeal to join the Cooperative and Economical Society of London in his newspaper, *The Economist,* on March 2, 1822. The society provided meals and cultural events as well as housing to its members in a communal building. Here Mudie revealed his views of the gender division of labor and his ideas about the place of child labor.

TO THE WORKING AND OTHER CLASSES:

New and grand Cooperation, affording ample security for your comfortable and abundant subsistence; for your support during sickness or loss of employment, and in old age; for the education and moral training of your children; their instruction in useful knowledge and productive industry, and their permanent support for life, in the event of the death of their parents. . . .

I. The families contribute to a common fund for providing the necessaries of life, at wholesale prices and at the best markets, in proportion to the number of individuals in each family. . . .

II. The families breakfast, dine etc. together at the general tables; and in the evenings amuse themselves with conversation, reading, lectures, music etc. in the public room. The individuals, however, are at perfect liberty, at all times, to take their meals, and to spend their leisure hours, in their private apartments.

III. The domestic duties of the females are performed under a system of combination, which greatly lessens their labor, and enables the females either to be profitably employed, or to command a considerable portion of leisure for rational pursuits and innocent recreations. Thus, the cooking for the whole of the families being performed at once and at one fire, occupies comparatively but a small portion of time, and is done in a much superior manner to what is possible for small individual families; and a proportionate advantage is gained in all other departments of housewifery, such as cleaning, washing, getting up linen, etc. etc. . . .

IV. Such of the females as are not required for the discharge of the duties of housewifery, and for the care of the children, are employed, during a moderate portion of the day, in such profitable work as can be obtained, for the benefit of the society at large. The elder children are also employed during six hours daily, for the common benefit, and will be carefully instructed in the

The clasped hands at the center of this banner of the Chicago union of German-American furniture workers (Moebel Arbeiter) symbolize fraternity and solidarity, and the branches surrounding them represent strength (oak) and peace (olive). The union, founded in Chicago in 1872, carried this banner during labor marches and demonstrations.

principles of Christianity, and in one or more branches of useful industry. The remainder of their time is occupied with their education, and such sports, under the care of their superintendents, as are suitable to their age. . . .

VI. The society already employs its own shoemakers and tailors, and will speedily be enabled to perform all its own work within itself. The society also can now promptly execute, for the public, in the best and cheapest manner, orders for carving and gilding, transparent landscape window blinds, paintings on velvet, boot and shoe-making, gentlemen's clothing, and dressmaking and millinery.

Among those who suffered the worst effects of industrialization, miners contributed to the call for reform by circulating pamphlets and broadsides that drew attention to the dreadful conditions in which they worked. An 1841 broadside published by a British miner dramatically compared the state of English workingmen to the condition of African slaves. The writer invoked the English love of liberty, implying that the "British slavery" of workingmen was even more intolerable than the enslavement of Africans in the British Caribbean. The writer tried to enlist the support of women and mothers to make his case against the employment of young children in the mines.

AN EARNEST ADDRESS, &c.

People of England,

. . . the cause I plead is the cause of your fellow subjects and fellow countrymen—yes it is the cause of BRITISH SLAVERY to which I beg to call your attention—a slavery much more oppressive and intolerable (though it may not, in some instances be so humiliating and degrading) than perhaps any regular establishment of African slaves in all the West Indies—I mean the case of thousands of your fellow-countrymen in the counties of Northumberland and Durham employed in the coal mines.

It is needless here to remind you . . . that you stand more indebted to the dauntless bravery and indefatigable industry of this great body of men, for the social and domestic enjoyments of your families and your firesides, than to the exertions of any one class of the British community. Thousands upon thousands of you, however, are totally unacquainted with the real situation of this most useful, yet most abused class of men. You have no real idea of the dangers they every moment stand exposed to, while procuring the fuel which comforts, cheers and enlivens you round your social hearths. Equally ignorant are you of the privations and hardship to which this body of men and their families are subjected by the avaricious cruelty of their ruthless, cold-hearted Egyptian Task-Masters. Comparatively few of you know that the Pitman before he can obtain a single particle of Coals, has to descend by a rope from five hundred to upwards of twelve hundred feet below the surface of the earth, down a cavern, so horribly terrific and frightful, that if all the Coal Pits in Europe and the entire Continent of America, into the bargain, were offered to some of those men, who claim them as their property, on condition of their having to be looped down by a rope to the bottom of those gulfs of destruction their dastard spirits would shudder; whilst they, with ghastly paleness, unhesitating, would reject the offer; knowing that such a descent might bring them *too near home!*

After the poor but brave Pitman descends to the bottom of this horrific cavern, he has however to walk, or rather crawl a mile, or perhaps two or three, through subterraneous vaults, where the "pestilence that walketh in darkness" hangs thick and heavy around him and at every step he is liable to be crushed to pieces by some ponderous body from the roof, whilst the slightest inadvertency or casualty in the most distant part of the Pit, might, and often has in an instant involved him and his fellow slaves in

I worked in a lower room, where I heard the proposed strike fully, if not vehemently discussed; I had been an ardent listener . . . and naturally, I took sides with the strikers. When the day came on which the girls were to turn out, those in the upper rooms started first, and so many of them left, that our mill was at once shut down. Then when the girls in my room stood irresolute, uncertain what to do, I, who began to think that they would not go out after all their talk, became impatient and started on ahead, saying with childish bravado, "I don't care what you do, I am going to turn out [strike], whether anyone else does or not;" and I marched out and was followed by the others."

— Harriet Robinson, account of 1834 strike in Lowell, Massachusetts

destruction, and in many instances left the mangled fragments of his body indistinguishable from those of scores of his fellow sufferers, but allowing him, amidst the ten thousand dangers that surround him, to reach in safety that point where

His efforts and energies must all be called into action, there, perhaps, under torrents of water, equal to any incessant shower bath, he often labours from ten to fifteen hours mid-thigh deep in water; the pernicious exhalations from which entail upon him a whole train of chronic diseases, and in some instances deprive him of sight, whilst the total absence of one breath of air fit for respiration, never fail to wear out, in a few years, the hardiest constitution. In other situations he has to extend himself at full length on his side, and in that position, for eight, ten, or twelve hours successively, to endure, and go through toil and labour that would probably kill the strongest horse in Europe—whilst the sweat falls from every pore of his body. For the sweat thus wrung from his body,—the marrow from his bones, and the blood from his veins, your humanity and generous feeling will lead you, in many instances, to conclude that the Pitman must be liberally paid and generously rewarded—but the very reverse is the case . . .

Thus situated, the poor Pitman's frame, in a few years, becomes exhausted, from excessive labour; and his eleven or twelve shillings a week, are found inadequate to keep soul and body together—especially where he happens to have a wife and half a dozen children depending on his labour. What is to be done? Why his very kind and tender-hearted employers, (*good creatures*) can better his condition by taking his dear infants into slavery, at the tender age of five or six years old. . . .

Oh! Ye British females, let me address those of you who know what it is to be mothers—think, for a moment, what would be your feelings to be compelled to drag your infant, five or six years of age, from its bed . . . to go to one of those yawning gulfs, at a distance of two or three miles from your residence, where it is to strive to protract its unfortunate existence by earning, in those terrific gulfs the means of purchasing [a] brown crust of bread!

In 1824, the British Parliament repealed the Combination Acts, passed in 1799 and 1800 to prevent workers from unionizing. English workers were now free to organize labor unions. These pioneers used unions to resist threats to their skills, status, and wages. In 1829, under the leadership of labor activist John Doherty, textile workers from throughout

Britain formed the Grand General Union of Operative Spinners. These resolutions suggested that workers wanted to protect jobs for spinners' families and outlaw child labor. They also wanted women to organize separately.

3. That one Grand General Union of all the Operative Spinners in the United Kingdom be now formed for the mutual support and protection of all. . . .

6. That all [males] capable of spinning be caused to pay one penny weekly, to the general fund as members of this association, and that in cases of strikes all such as remain out shall receive the same allowance as the spinner . . .

8. That 10 shillings a week be paid to members when contending for an advance of wages the same as when resisting reductions, but that no district or part of a district be allowed to strike for an advance without first having obtained the consent and authority of the other districts. . . .

18. That no person or persons be learned or allowed to spin after the 5th of April 1830 except the son, brother or orphan nephew of spinners, and the poor relations of the proprietors of the mills, and those only when they have attained the full age of 15 years; such persons being instructed or allowed to spin only when the spinner is in the wheelhouse following the wheels and attending to the work. Any person acting contrary to this shall be fined for the first offence in the sum of half a guinea, for the second one guinea, and for the third to be expelled from the society and have his name exposed throughout the whole trade.

24. That female spinners be urged to become members of an association to be formed exclusively for themselves, and that an entrance ceremony be prepared for them suited to their circumstances, and that they pay into and receive from their own fund such sum or sums as they may from time to time agree upon and they receive all the aid of the whole confederation in supporting them to obtain men's prices, or such remuneration for their labour as may be deemed sufficient under general or particular circumstances. . . .

27. That it is not the intention of this Association either directly or indirectly to interfere with, or in any way injure the rights and property of employers or to assume or exercise any control or authority over the management of any mill or mills, but, on the contrary, will endeavour as far as in us lies to uphold the just rights and reasonable authority of every master.

Working men in London circulated this announcement to establish the Metropolitan Trades' Union in March, 1831. One of their goals was to get rid of voting rules that allowed only men who owned property to vote.

FELLOW WORKMEN,
. . . the first great evil that stands in the way of bettering our condition, is, that we, the working people of England, are UNREPRESENTED! totally destitute of political influence in the Great Council of the Nation! . . . Are you content to remain the degraded victims of such an unjust system? . . . We earnestly hope not. Let us henceforth adopt and practice a new principle;— instead of every man being for himself exclusively, let us, in future, be ALL for EACH, and EACH for ALL. To do this, the intelligence and energy of the working classes must be concentrated; and it is, therefore, proposed THAT A METROPOLITAN TRADES' UNION be formed. Its first object, to obtain, for all its members, the right of electing those who make the laws which govern them, unshackled and uninfluenced by any Property Qualification whatsoever. Its second object, to afford support and protection, individually and collectively, to every member of the METROPOLITAN TRADES' UNION; to enhance the value of labor by diminishing the hours of employment; and to adopt such measures as may be deemed necessary to increase the domestic comforts of working men.

Socialism and Revolution

Socialist thinkers also addressed the problem of inequality between social classes. One of them, a Frenchman, Louis Blanc, argued in his 1840 book, *The Organization of Labor,* that competition between workers for scarce jobs drove down wages and had to be eliminated. Blanc proposed that governments take the lead by providing work for all in what he called "social workshops." The government, rather than private employers, would regulate work and workers would keep the profits from their labor. Blanc envisioned setting up workshops in every industry.

What does competition mean to workingmen? Is it the distribution of work to the highest bidder? A contractor needs a laborer: three apply. "How much do you ask for your work?" "Three francs, I have a wife and children." "Good, and you?" "Two and a half francs. I have no children but a wife." So much the better, and you? "Two francs will do for me; I am single." "You shall have the work." With this the affair is settled; the bargain is closed. What will become now of the other two proletarians? They will starve it is to be hoped. But what if they become thieves? Never mind, why have we our police? Or murderers? Well, for them we have the gallows. And the fortunate one of the three; even his victory is only temporary. Let a fourth laborer appear, strong enough to fast one out of every two days; the desire to cut down the wages will be exerted to its fullest extent. A new pariah, perhaps a new recruit for the galleys. . . .

Who would be blind enough not to see that under the reign of free competition the continuous decline of wages necessarily becomes a general law with no exception whatsoever? . . . A systematic lowering of wages resulting in the elimination of a certain number of laborers is the inevitable effect of free competition. . . .

The government ought to be considered as the supreme regulator of production and endowed for this duty with great power.

This task would consist of fighting competition and of finally overcoming it.

The government . . . should erect social workshops in the most important branches of national industry.

All workmen who can give guarantee of morality shall be called to work in these social workshops up to the limit of the original capital gathered together for the purchase of tools. . . .

If the social workshops were once established according to these principles, you could easily understand what the results could be. In every great industry, in machinery for example, or the silk or cotton industry, or in printing establishments, the social workshops would be in competition with private industries. Would the fight be a long one? No, for the social workshops would have advantages over the others, the results of the cheaper communal life and through the organization by which all laborers, without exception, are interested in producing good and quick work.

Major socialist figures appear on this poster for the French socialist newspaper La Petite République *(The Little Republic). Workers plow the soil and sow seeds, implying that the socialists appealed to rural as well as to urban workers. The woman in flowing robes and hat in the center represents Marianne, the traditional symbol of the French republic.*

The two most famous critics of industrial capitalism, Karl Marx and Frederick Engels, took a more extreme view than either trade unionists or early socialist thinkers. In their revolutionary work, *The Communist Manifesto,* written in the heady atmosphere of the European-wide revolutions of 1848, which demanded democratic governments and constitutions, Marx and Engels argued that a more just society could only emerge from a radical change in the economic order. The *Manifesto* was not only an analysis of the development of capitalism, but also a call to action; it ended with the stirring words, "Workers unite! You have nothing to lose but your chains!" In the *Manifesto,* Marx and Engels described the widening gap between the bourgeoisie (employers) and the proletariat (workers).

Society as a whole is more and more splitting up into two great hostile camps, into two great classes directly facing each other: Bourgeoisie and Proletariat. . . .

Each step in the development of the bourgeoisie was accompanied by a corresponding political advance of that class. . . . the bourgeoisie has at last, since the establishment of Modern Industry and of the world market, conquered for itself, in the modern representative State, exclusive political sway. The executive of

Karl Marx, German political and economic theorist, and co-author with Frederick Engels of the Communist Manifesto. *Marx and Engels argued that industrial capitalism would exploit the working class, but that eventually workers would revolt against their capitalist employers.*

the modern State is but a committee for managing the common affairs of the whole bourgeoisie. . . .

The bourgeosie cannot exist without constantly revolutionizing the instruments of production, and thereby the relations of production, and with them the whole relations of society. Conservation of the old modes of production in unaltered form was, on the contrary, the first condition of existence for earlier industrial classes. Constant revolutionizing of production, uninterrupted disturbance of all social conditions, everlasting uncertainty and agitation distinguish the bourgeois epoch from all earlier ones. The need of a constantly expanding market for its products chases the bourgeoisie over the whole surface of the globe. It must nestle everywhere, settle everywhere, establish connections everywhere.

In proportion as the bourgeoisie . . . is developed, in the same proportion is the proletariat, the modern working class developed—a class of labourers, who live only so long as they find work, and who find work only so long as their labour increases capital. These labourers, who must sell themselves piecemeal, are a commodity like every other article of commerce, and are consequently exposed to all the vicissitudes of competition, to all the fluctuations of the market.

Owing to the extensive use of machinery and to division of labour, the work of the proletarians has lost all individual character, and, consequently, all charm, for the workman. He becomes an appendage of the machine, and it is only the most simple, most monotonous, and most easily acquired knack, that is required of him. Hence, the cost of production of a workman is restricted, almost entirely, to the means of subsistence that he requires for his maintenance, and for the propagation of his race. But the price of a commodity, and therefore also of labour, is equal to its cost of production. In proportion therefore, as the repulsiveness of the work increases, the wage decreases. Nay more, in proportion as the use of machinery and division of labour increases, in the same proportion the burden of toil also increases, whether by prolongation of the working hours, by increase of the work exacted in a given time or by increased speed of the machinery, etc.

Modern industry has converted the little workshop of the patriarchal master into the great factory of the industrial capitalist. Masses of labourers, crowded into the factory, are organized like soldiers. As privates of the industrial army they are placed under the command of a perfect hierarchy of officers and sergeants. Not only are they slaves of the bourgeois class, and of the bourgeois State; they are daily and hourly enslaved by the machine, by the overlooker, and, above all, by the individual bourgeois manufacturer himself. The more openly this despotism proclaims gain to be its end and aim, the more petty, the more hateful and the more embittering it is. . . .

Of all the classes that stand face to face with the bourgeoisie today, the proletariat alone is a really revolutionary class.

International Movements

The development of trade unions inspired Marx, along with others who shared his views to form an international socialist organization to advance the aims of the working class on a global scale. Established in London in 1864, the International Working Men's Association emphasized working-class solidarity and organization in trade unions. Marx believed that the working class had to organize economically before it could hope to seize control of political institutions. In addition to British trade union leaders, members came from the ranks of foreign labor activists who had fled to London to escape repression in their own countries. The declaration of the International Working Men's Association (IWMA) clearly reflected the views of Marx and Engels set forth sixteen years earlier in the *Communist Manifesto*.

CONSIDERING,

That the emancipation of the working classes must be conquered by the working- classes themselves; that the struggle for the emancipation of the working classes means not a struggle for class privileges and monopolies, but for equal rights and duties, and the abolition of all class rule;

That the economical subjection of the man of labor to the monopoliser of the means of labor, that is, the sources of life, lies at the bottom of servitude in all its forms, of all social misery, mental degradation and political dependence;

That the economical emancipation of the working classes is therefore the great end to which every political movement ought to be subordinate as a means;

That all efforts aiming at that great end have hitherto failed from . . . the absence of a fraternal bond of union between the working classes of different countries;

That the emancipation of labor is neither a local, nor a national, but a social problem, embracing all countries in which modern

"National differences and antagonisms between peoples are daily more and more vanishing, owing to the development of the bourgeoisie, to freedom of commerce, to the world market, to uniformity in the mode of production, and in the conditions of life corresponding thereto."

—Karl Marx and
Frederick Engels,
The Communist Manifesto, 1848

society exists, and depending for its solution on the concurrence practical and theoretical, of the most advanced countries;

That the present revival of the working classes in the most industrious countries of Europe, while it raises a new hope, gives solemn warning against a relapse into the old errors, and calls for the immediate combination of the still discontented movements;

FOR THESE REASONS,

The first International Working Men's Congress declares that the International Association and, all societies and individuals adhering to it will acknowledge truth, justice, and morality, as the basis of their conduct towards each other, and towards all men without regard to color, creed, or nationality.

This Congress considers it the duty of a man to claim the rights of a man and a citizen, not only for himself, but for every man who does his duty. No rights without duties, no duties without rights.

In 1871, a French transportation worker, Eugene Pottier, wrote the words to the song, "L'Internationale," and in 1888, Pierre Degeyter, a wood worker, set them to music. Unions and radical movements around the world adopted it as a standard anthem. These stanzas are from the version translated from the French by Charles Kerr in 1901.

Arise ye prisoners of starvation!
Arise ye wretched of the earth,
For justice thunders condemnation,
A better world's in birth
No more tradition's chains shall bind us,
Arise ye slaves, no more in thrall!
The earth shall rise on new foundations,
We have been naught, we shall be all.

Refrain

Tis the final conflict
Let each stand in his place
The Industrial Union
Shall be the human race.

We want no condescending saviors,
To rule us from a judgement hall;
We workers ask not for their favors;
Let us consult for all.

To make the thief disgorge his booty
To free the spirit from its cell,
We must ourselves decide our duty,
We must decide and do it well.

Refrain

The law oppresses us and tricks us,
Wage systems drain our blood;
The rich are free from obligations,
The laws the poor delude.
Too long we've languished in subjection,
Equality has other laws;
"No rights," says she "without their duties,
No claims on equals without cause."

The visible social inequalities, such as those between rich and poor, that the industrial revolution produced led other thinkers to advocate an extreme form of freedom and the rejection of all formal institutions, religion, political parties, and even governments. These thinkers called themselves "anarchists." Anarchists rejected what they believed were the authoritarian tendencies of the Marxists who led the International Working Men's Association and eventually they left the IWMA. One anarchist, Russian Mikhail Bakunin, set forth his vision of anarchism in his "Revolutionary Catechism," published in 1866.

II. Replacing the cult of God by respect and love of humanity, we proclaim human reason as the only criterion of truth; human conscience as the basis of justice; individual and collective freedom as the only source of order in society.

III. Freedom is the absolute right of every adult man and woman to seek no other sanction for their acts than their own conscience and their own reason, being responsible first to themselves and then to the society which they have voluntarily accepted. . . .

V. The freedom of each is therefore realizable only in the equality of all. The realization of freedom through equality, in principle and in fact, is justice. . . .

VII. Absolute rejection of every authority including that which sacrifices freedom for the convenience of the state. . . . The political and economic structure of society must now be reorganized

Men wave flags with the names of working-class political parties from around the world on the sheet music for the socialist anthem "The Internationale." The absence of women in this image hint at men's ambivalence about their role in the movement.

on the basis of freedom. Henceforth, order in society must result from the greatest possible realization of individual liberty, as well as of liberty on all levels of social organization.

VIII. The political and economic organization of social life must not, as at present, be directed from the summit to the base—the center to the circumference—imposing unity through forced centralization. On the contrary, it must be reorganized to issue from the base to the summit—from the circumference to the center—according to the principles of free association and federation.

However, without certain absolutely essential conditions the practical realization of freedom will be forever impossible.

These conditions are:

A. The abolition of all state religions and all privileged churches, including those partially maintained or supported by state subsidies. Absolute liberty of every religion to build temples to their gods, and to pay and support their priests. . . .

C. Abolition of monarchy; establishment of a commonwealth.

D. Abolition of classes, ranks, and privileges; absolute equality of political rights for all men and women; universal suffrage.

E. Abolition, dissolution, and moral, political, and economic dismantling of the all-pervasive, regimented, centralized State, the alter ego of the Church, and as such, the permanent cause of the impoverishment, brutalization, and enslavement of the multitude. This naturally entails the following: Abolition of all state universities: public education must be administered only by the communes and free associations. Abolition of the state judiciary: all judges must be elected by the people. Abolition of all criminal, civil, and legal codes now administered in Europe: because the code of liberty can be created only by liberty itself. Abolition of banks and all other institutions of state credit. Abolition of all centralized administration, of the bureaucracy, of all permanent armies and state police. . . .

Women's Place: Home or Factory?

Despite their progressive, if not revolutionary, political aims, men within the ranks of organized labor in both Europe and America held traditional views of women's place in the labor force and in society. Although they recognized that women were among the most exploited and underpaid workers, many believed that women belonged at home, not in the factory, views that they expressed in speeches to the September

7, 1866, meeting of the International Working Men's Association. The minutes of that meeting show that the first speaker argued that women could contribute to the civic health of a democratic republic through their domestic activities. Not all the members agreed that women should be prevented from working, however.

M. Coullery . . . paints a somber picture of woman's miseries, of the insufficient resources she obtains through her labors, of the ensuing demoralization, of the painful work for which she is not equipped and that perverts her sex; of the temptations and traps that...the corrupt parasitic class [the middle class or bourgeoisie] sets out for her. Woman's place is in the home, near her children: she should watch over them and instruct them in the first principles [of life]. She has a great mission; if we give her the place she deserves and if we cast off evil influences, she will become very foundation of liberty and democracy.

MM. Chemalé, Tolain, Fribourg, of the French delegation, propose [that]: From the physical, moral, and social point of view women's [wage] labor must be vigorously condemned as the principal [cause] of the degeneration of the race and as one of the capitalist class's agents of demoralization. Nature has endowed woman with predetermined functions: her place is in the family! Her job is raising children during their early years. The mother alone is capable of fulfilling this task.

They cite statistics that confirm the mortality of children abandoned to wet-nurses or day-care. The mother alone is capable of giving the child a moral education, of forming a responsible man. Moreover, the woman is the tie and the attraction that keeps the man at home, gives him habits of order and morality. . . . This is woman's real work; it is a terrible mistake to impose another on her.

MM. Varlin and Bourdon . . . propose [that]: lack of education, excess labor, insufficient wages and the poor hygiene of factories are the causes of physical and moral degradation. These [evils] can be eliminated by a better organization of labor and by cooperation. Because women need to work in order to live decently we must seek ways of improving their work, not suppressing it.

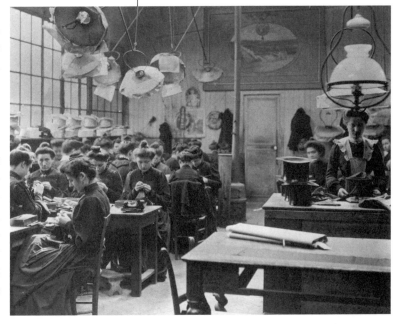

Women stitch hats in this New York City factory around 1900. A small stove in the center of the room provides the only heat in cold weather, but compared to the conditions in which many workers labored, this factory seems relatively clean, orderly, and well lit.

In the United States, Edward O'Donnell, a member of the American Federation of Labor (AFL), the umbrella organization that grouped all unions of skilled workers, spoke out against women's work in 1897 in the AFL newspaper, The American Federationist.

The rapid displacement of men by women in the factory and workshop has to be met sooner or later, and the question is forcing itself upon the leaders and thinkers among the labor organizations of the land.

Is it a pleasing indication of progress to see the father, the brother and the son displaced as the bread winner by the mother, sister and daughter?

Is not this evolutionary backslide, which certainly modernizes the present wage system in vogue, a menace to prosperity—a foe to our civilized pretensions?

The growing demand for female labor is not founded upon philanthropy, as those who encourage it would have sentimentalists believe; it does not spring from the milk of human kindness. It is an insidious assault upon the home; it is the knife of the assassin, aimed at the family circle—the divine injunction. It debars the man through financial embarrassment from family responsibility, and physically, mentally and socially excludes the woman equally from nature's dearest impulse. . . .

The wholesale employment of women in the various handicrafts must gradually unsex them, as it most assuredly is demoralizing them, or stripping them of that modest demeanor that lends a charm to their kind, while it numerically strengthens the multitudinous army of loafers, paupers, tramps and policemen.

This proposition is rejected by the majority, which adopts MM. Chemalé's and Tolain's proposition.

The Congress . . . [condemns] in principal women's factory labor as one of the causes of the degeneration and demoralization of the human race. . . .

Paule Minck, French labor activist and socialist, forcefully defended women's right to work in this speech made at a public meeting in Paris on July 13, 1868. Minck argued that the answer to women's exploitation in the industrial system was not to banish them from the workplace, but to secure better working conditions and higher wages for them. Moreover, Minck pointed out, work could give women a sense of self-worth and control over their lives.

And would you like to suppress all work other than reproduction for women?

. . . I am speaking here about appropriate work, not the abusive exploitation that turns all workers and especially the poor woman into a slave, the serf of modern society, at the mercy and misery of speculation.

Work is a necessary law, which we must all obey. . . . Everything in nature stirs itself and works; and it is the union of these activities, of these diverse aptitudes, that produces good and creates the sublime harmony of all beings and things.

It is said that work exhausts and kills . . . Must one . . . conclude that because women work too much that therefore they should not work at all, and let them avoid the exhaustion produced by excessive work by plunging them into enervation caused by idleness?

Let us work to raise women's salaries, to ensure that they are commensurate with what is produced, raise them in proportion to the cost of life's necessities and there will be no excess, no sapping of strength of the kind that inevitably leads to corruption, degeneration, and even death.

It is said that women's excessive work causes the bastardization of the race. Certainly, excessive work—whether by woman or man—is an atrocious anomaly that must disappear; but we believe that the degeneration of the race owes more to excessive vice and the depravity produced by the unjust distribution of women's salaries, which inevitably leads to debauchery and all its evils. . . .

It is certainly essential that women produce goods and earn money, but it does not follow that her work will only lower men's wages. Equal pay for equal work, this is the only true justice. One must not base wages on the needs of the worker, but on the worker's production. It is about time that the scandalous anomaly of wage differences [between men and women] disappears forever. And is it not odious that under the specious pretext that women have fewer needs than men that [employers] authorize themselves to pay them two, three, and even four times less than men?

In the United States, African-American women experienced double discrimination: the majority of unions refused to admit them on the grounds of both their race and their sex. As a result, African Americans formed their own labor organizations. In 1866, Washerwomen of Jackson, Mississippi, a black women's organization, wrote a letter to the mayor of Jackson asking him to intervene in helping them raise their wages. The letter was published in Jackson's newspaper, *The Daily Clarion*.

Jackson, Miss., June 20, 1866

Mayor Barrows—Dear Sir:

At a meeting of the colored Washerwomen of the city on the evening of the 18th of June, the subject of raising the wages was considered, and owing to many circumstances, the following preamble and resolution were unanimously adopted:

Whereas, under the influence of the present high prices of all the necessaries of life, and the attendant high rates of rent, while our wages remain very much reduced, we, the washerwomen of the city of Jackson, State of Mississippi, thinking it impossible to life uprightly and honestly in laboring for the present daily and monthly recompense, and hoping meet with the support of all good citizens, join in adopting unanimously the following resolution:

Be it resolved by the washerwomen of this city and county, that on and after the foregoing date, we join in charging a uniform rate for our labor, that rate being an advance over the original price by the month or day the statement of said price to be made public by printing the same, and anyone belonging to the class of washerwomen violating this, shall be liable to a fine *regulated by [our organization]*.

We do not wish in the least to charge exorbitant prices, but desire to be able to live comfortably if possible from the fruits of our labor.

We present the matter to your Honor, and hope you will not reject it as the condition of prices call on us to raise our wages.

During an 1898 strike, the Chicago-Virden Coal Company attempted to hire African American men as strikebreakers by placing this advertisement in a Birmingham, Alabama, newspaper. When the strikebreakers arrived in Chicago, violence broke out between white strikers and black strikebreakers, killing twelve people and wounding several more.

The prices charged are:

$1.50 per day for washing

$15.00 per month for family washing

$10.00 per month for single individuals

We ask you to consider the matter in our behalf, and should you deem it just and right, your sanction of the movement will be greatly received.

Yours, very truly,
The Washerwomen of Jackson

Strike!

Over the course of the nineteenth century, workers struck employers, attempting to shorten working hours and increase their wages. Women were frequently active strikers. In 1860, for example, in one of the largest pre–Civil War strikes in the United States, women shoemakers struck in Lynn, Massachusetts, for shorter hours and higher wages. Eventually, individual states in the United States established the eight-hour day beginning in the 1860s; in Europe, eight-hour legislation lagged. In August 1903, German textile workers, including many women, in the town of Crimmitschau in Saxony went on strike for a ten-hour day and circulated this tract, appealing to the townspeople for support and indicating how the strike could hurt local businesses.

The manufacturers of Crimmitschau are provoking a trial of strength.

The worker is to be brought to his knees. Beaten and defenseless, he is to be kept down after an unequal battle. It is the intention of the manufacturers to sit on their money bags and starve out the workers. They began their infamous action by a miserable breach of agreement; lies and misrepresentations followed. . . . The conditional notice by the workers of five factories was followed by the employers with the brutal sacking of 7,000 industrious workers of both sexes.

The whole world looks upon this mass dismissal as a brutal coup, a provocation of the workers. And what are they doing now? Now they expect these same 7,000 workers to come crawling before the thrones of the manufacturers and declare themselves willing to work under the old conditions. What bitter mockery! What a slap in the face of the workers! They want to

Seamstresses Take Action

Six years after the Crimmitschau strike in Germany, and after several years during which labor unions in New York City had tried to organize women shirtwaist makers, a major conflict paralyzed the New York garment industry. When garment manufacturers refused to allow workers to form labor unions, beginning in November, 1909, 20,000 shirtwaist makers, most of them immigrant women, went on strike, shutting down one garment factory after another.

degrade the workers into slaves, into men without honour! This is what the workers would have to be, to accept such an insinuation. The worker would rather be defeated after a hard battle, when all his powers are exhausted, than accept such an offer.

Thus, you people of Crimmitschau, thus do the manufacturers of Crimmitschau act! . . . If in the next months you stand idly behind your counter in your shop because the workers have to be economical in their purchases; if you don't know where to turn in meeting your bills because your customers are staying away, you can thank the manufacturers for it! . . .

The question of the 10-hour day has nothing to do with politics. It is a question of humanity and its introduction is a commandment of humanity. Listen, citizens of our town, to how a bourgeois paper, the *Arbeitsmarkt-Korrespondenz*, comments on the 10-hour day:

> The Chief Inspector for Baden considers 11 hours standing at work, necessary in spinning and weaving, as highly harmful to the female physique. According to the observations of doctors, a large proportion of female textile workers who work 11 hours a day . . . are chronically overtired; they mostly also look poorly. . . . A whole series of inspectors [have] demanded the limitation of hours for female textile workers to 10 a day.

What all doctors, all experts in social medicine, all reasonable human beings . . . recognize without reservation, our Crimmitschau mill-owners are too blind to see. Why is the mill-worker, in spite of his easy work, weaker and physically less developed than the agricultural worker? . . . Because his constitution deteriorates in the monotonous work of the mill and in its dusty atmosphere. . . . the work of the hand-loom weavers of 100 years ago, using all the muscles of the body, did less damage than employment in the factory today.

Strikes sometimes turned violent and even deadly, illustrating the intensity of conflicts between workers, employees, and police. In January 1912, textile workers in the town of

Organizers of a strike in London in 1889 called upon both men and women to protest "sweating" in the tailoring trades. Strike organizers encouraged workers to take action against the practice of paying them scanty piece rates or weekly rates to work long hours in filthy conditions in order to make a living wage.

Lawrence, Massachusetts, made history when they shut down factories after employers cut their wages. Ironically, their cut wages were a result of new legislation passed by the state of Massachusetts reducing the length of the workday for women and children. The Industrial Workers of the World (IWW), a militant labor organization devoted to organizing unskilled and immigrant workers, led the strike, which lasted for three months. In her autobiography, *The Rebel Girl*, IWW organizer Elizabeth Gurley Flynn described its course. The strike was exceptionally violent, with clashes between strikers and police. In one such clash, a woman striker, Anna La Pizza, was killed.

The strike broke with dramatic suddenness on January 11, 1912, the first payday of the year. A law reducing the hours of women and children under 18, from 56 hours a week to 54 had been passed by the Massachusetts legislature. It affected the majority of the employees. The employers had strongly resisted the passage of this law. Now they cut the pay proportionately in the first pay envelope. Wages were already at the starvation point. The highest paid weavers received $10.50 weekly. Spinners, carders, spoolers and others averaged $6 to $7 weekly. Whole families worked in the mills to eke out a bare existence. Pregnant women worked at the machines until a few hours before their babies were born. Sometimes a baby came right there in the mill, between the looms. The small pittance taken from the workers . . . was the spark that ignited the general strike. "Better to starve fighting than to starve working!" became their battle-cry. It spread from mill to mill. In a few hours of that cold, snowy day in January, 14,000 workers poured out of the mills. In a few days the mills were empty and still—and remained so for nearly three months.

It was estimated that there were at least 25 different nationalities in Lawrence. The largest groups among the strikers were: Italians, 7,000; Germans, 6,000; French Canadians, 5,000; all English speaking, 5,000; Poles, 2,500; Lithuanians, 2,000; Franco-Belgians, 1,100; Syrians, 1,000—with a sprinkling of Russians, Jews, Greeks, Letts and Turks. The local IWW became the organizing core of the strike. . . . [it] organized mass meetings in various localities of the different language groups and had them elect a strike committee of men and women which represented every mill, every department and every nationality. They held meetings of all the strikers together on the Lawrence Common . . . so that the workers could realize their oneness and strength. . . . There

As a labor organizer for the International Workers of the World (IWW), Elizabeth Gurley Flynn was a radical firebrand. What made the IWW unique, according to Flynn, was that it tried to organize all workers into "One Big Union, regardless of skill or lack of it, foreign-born or native-born, color, religion or sex."

were 1,400 state militiamen in Lawrence, which was like an armed camp. Clashes occurred daily between the strikers and the police and state troopers. . . .

A proposal was made by some of the strikers that we adopt a method used successfully in Europe—to send the children out of Lawrence to be cared for in other cities. The parents accepted the idea and the children were wild to go. On February 17, 1912, the first group of 150 children were taken to New York City. A small group also left for Barre, Vermont.

On February 24, 1912, a group of 40 strikers' children were to go from Lawrence to Philadelphia . . . At the railroad station in Lawrence, where the children were assembled accompanied by their fathers and mothers, just as they were ready to board the train they were surrounded by police. Troopers surrounded the station outside to keep others out. Children were clubbed and torn away from their parents and a wild scene of brutal disorder took place. Thirty-five frantic women and children were arrested, thrown screaming and fighting into patrol wagons. They were beaten into submission and taken to the police station. There the women were charged with "neglect" and improper guardianship and ten frightened children were taken to the Lawrence Poor Farm. . . . It was a day without parallel in American labor history.

Governments Take Action

Working people and labor-movement leaders were not the only ones to protest industrial exploitation. From the beginning of the nineteenth century, government officials and reformers worked to expose the harsh conditions of labor. Michael Sadler, chair of the parliamentary commission investigating child labor, made a passionate speech for child-labor reform in the summer of 1832. Sadler recognized that many employers objected to regulatory legislation on the grounds that such laws would interfere with the ability of working people and employers to form contracts on their own accord.

But, he asserted, children were too young to be considered free agents and the freedom of contract objection had little weight. The Factory Act of 1833 restricted the hours of children between ages nine and thirteen and of those below eighteen, and required employers to allow children to attend school for at least two hours during every workday.

The Bill which I now implore the House to sanction with its authority, has for its object the liberation of children and other young persons employed in the mills and factories of the United Kingdom, from that over-exertion and long confinement which common sense, as well as experience, has shown to be utterly inconsistent with the improvement of their minds, the preservation of their morals, and the maintenance of their health—in a word, to rescue them from a state of suffering and degradation, which it is conceived the children of the industrious classes in hardly any other country has ever endured. . . .

I apprehend, that the strongest objections that will be offered on this occasion, will be grounded upon the pretence that the very principle of the Bill is an improper interference between the employer and the employed, and an attempt to regulate by law the market of labour. Were the market supplied by free agents, properly so denominated, I should fully participate in these objections . . . but children, at all events, are not to be regarded as free labourers. The common-place objections that the parents are free agents, and that the children therefore ought to be regarded as such, I apprehend has but little force. . . .

The parents who surrender their children to this infantile slavery . . . are obliged, by extreme indigence, so to act, but . . . do it with great reluctance and bitter regret: themselves perhaps out of employment to working at very low wages, and their families in a state of great destitution;—what can they do? The overseer refuses relief if they have children capable of working in factories whom they object to send thither. They choose therefore what they probably deem the lesser evil, and reluctantly resign their offspring to the captivity and pollution of the mill; they rouse them in the winter morning, which, as a poor father says before the Lords Committee, they "feel very sorry to do"; they receive them fatigued and exhausted, many a weary hour after the day has closed; they see them droop and sicken, and in many cases, become cripples and die, before they reach their prime: and they do all this because they must otherwise suffer unrelieved, and

Striking Violence

When workers in the United States and in Europe demonstrated for the eight-hour day, violence often erupted. On May 4, 1886, a peaceful meeting for the eight-hour day at Haymarket Square in Chicago was the scene of tragedy when someone threw a bomb into a group of police and an exchange of gunfire produced several deaths. In 1891, in the industrial town of Fourmies, France, ten people were killed and eighty were injured when the army fired on workers peacefully demonstrating.

starve amidst their starving children. It is a mockery to contend that these parents have a choice . . . Free agents! To suppose that parents are free agents while dooming their flesh and blood to this fate, is to believe them monsters. . . . The idea of treating children and especially the children of the poor—above all, the children of the poor imprisoned in factories—as free agents, is too absurd . . . The protection of poor children and young persons from these hardships and cruelties to which their age and condition have always rendered them peculiarly liable, has ever been held one of the first and most important duties of every Christian legislature.

> ### FACTORIES.
>
> #### CORRESPONDENCE relative to the Firm of *Taylor, Ibbotson & Co.*
>
> My Lord, in the case of Taylor, Ibbotson & Co. I took the evidence from the mouths of the boys themselves. They stated to me that they commenced working on Friday morning, the 27th of May last, at six A.M., and that, with the exception of meal hours and one hour at midnight extra, they did not cease working till four o'clock on Saturday evening, having been two days and a night thus engaged. Believing the case scarcely possible, I asked every boy the same questions, and from each received the same answers. I then went into the house to look at the time book, and, in the presence of one of the masters, referred to the cruelty of the case, and stated that I should certainly punish it with all the severity in my power. Mr. Rayner, the certificating surgeon of Bastile, was with me at the time.

In a report written for a Parliamentary factory commission in 1836, a British factory inspector expresses shock at the fact that young boys had worked from six AM until four the next morning. Although the conditions in this factory were especially severe, this sort of exploitation of children at work was common.

Legislators in the United States lagged behind their European counterparts in regulating factory labor. The New England Working Men's Association, which agitated for the ten-hour day for both men and women in all industries in the 1840s, made one of the first attempts to reform legislation. In 1845, the members presented a petition to the Massachusetts state legislatures to limit hours and reform working conditions in textile mills. In spite of eloquent testimony on behalf of the young men and women operatives, legislators rejected their appeal for a shorter working day. Legislators showed that one of their main concerns was that regulation would damage the competitive position of Massachusetts manufacturers. They preferred to leave the matter up to workers to negotiate with individual employers.

We have come to the conclusion *unanimously* that legislation is not necessary at the present time, and for the following reasons: . . .

2d. [The Committee believes] that the factory system, as it is called, is not more injurious to health than other kinds of indoor labor. That a law which would compel all of the factories in Massachusetts to run their machinery but ten hours out of the 24, while those in Maine, New Hampshire, Rhode Island, and other States in the Union were not restricted at all, the effect would be to close the gate of every mill in the State. It would be the same as closing our mills one day in every week, and although Massachusetts capital, enterprise, and industry are willing to

Photographic Investigation made by Lewis W. Hine in April and May, 1911. (Photographs and labels accompany this report.)

I.

From April 25th to May 16th 1911, I made quiet visits to every cotton mill in the state, with but one or two exceptions, and in all cases spending some time inside the mills during working-hours, as well as other hours spent around the mills at noon-hours, and around the homes at various times. In some of the villages, I made a careful house-to-house canvass, locating the homes of the working children and getting data about them.

I found ten cotton mills and one knitting mill running. The four largest in the state have been closed down from one to two years. The State Textile School was well worth the visit.

II. Meridian, Miss.

1. The Priscilla Knitting Mills, Meridian, Miss.

This mill, employing about 125 hands, is located out on the edge of town. Many of the workers came from the Meridian Cotton Mill, (a large mill, see Mr. Seddon's report, 1907), since it closed down. Photos #1349, 1449, 1489, 1967, #2006, 2011, #2030, #2031, show most of the youngest workers, and also the group of children under sixteen years who go home at 5:30 P.M., reducing their hours from 63 1/2 to 60. (See photo labels for names of children, etc.)

The National Child Labor Committee was formed in 1904 to campaign for legislation outlawing and regulating child labor. In this 1911 report, the committee reveals that even after child labor laws were passed, employers found ways to avoid compliance. The report also suggested that parents often condoned child labor.

compete on fair terms with the same of other States, and if needs be, with European nations, yet it is easy to perceive that we could not compete with our sister States, much less with foreign countries, if a restriction of this nature was put upon our manufactories.

3d. It would be impossible to legislate to restrict the hours of labor without affecting very materially the question of wages; and this is a matter which experience has taught us can be much better regulated by the parties themselves than by the Legislature. Labor in Massachusetts is a very different commodity from what it is in foreign countries. Here labor is on an equality with capital, and indeed controls it, and so it ever will be while free education and free constitutions exist. And although we may find fault and say that labor works too many hours, and labor is too severely tasked, yet if we attempt by legislation to enter within its orbit and interfere with its plans, we will be told to keep clear and to mind our own business. Labor is intelligent enough to make its own bargains, and look out for its own interests without any interference from us; and your Committee want no better proof to convince them that Massachusetts men and Massachusetts women are equal to this and will take care of themselves better than we can take care of them, than we had from the intelligent and virtuous men and women who appeared in support of this petition, before the committee.

4th. The Committee do not wish to be understood as conveying the impression that there are no abuses in the present system of labor; we think there are abuses; we think that many improvements may be made, and we believe will be made, by which labor will not be so severely tasked as it now is. We think that it would be better if the hours for labor were less,—if more time were allowed for meals, if more attention were paid to ventilation and pure air in our manufactories, and workshops, and many other matters. We acknowledge all this, but we say that the remedy is not with us. We look for it in the progressive improvement in art and science, in a higher appreciation of man's destiny, in a less love for money, and a more ardent love for social happiness and intellectual superiority.

By the 1890s, social activists in the United States stepped up the pressure for laws to ban child labor, working to get individual states to pass legislation. Florence Kelley, lawyer, Illinois factory inspector, and president of the National Consumer's League, was instrumental in getting the state of Illinois to pass an eight-hour law for children in 1893. Employers bitterly fought the law and, in 1895, the Illinois Supreme Court struck it down as unconstitutional. Before that happened, Kelley submitted a report to the state legislature discussing why it was so difficult to enforce the eight-hour law.

Although the law prohibits absolutely the employment of any child under 14 years of age in manufacture, yet the children under 14 years can never be wholly kept out of the factories and workshops until they are kept in school. At present the school attendance law is almost useless, at least in Chicago, where the largest number of children [has] been found at work. Although the Chicago Board of Education employs attendance agents, yet children leave school to sell papers; to carry cash in stores and telegrams and messages in streets; to peddle, black boots, "tend the baby," or merely to idle about. Unruly children are expelled from school to suit the convenience of teachers. Principals of schools have sent to the inspectors children 11 years old with the written request that permits be granted to enable the children to go to work (in violation of the factory law) because in each case the child is "incorrigible." As no factory can be a better place for a child 11 years old than a reasonably good school, this request voices the desire of the principal to be relieved of the trouble of the child. For all these various reasons, and perhaps also because of the want of sufficient school accommodations, children are freed from school attendance. . .

: . . . hundreds are seeking work in shops and factories and when they find work and the laws of the state are thereby violated, the task of prosecution, which should fall in part at least on the Board of Education of Chicago, devolves upon the State Factory Inspectors alone.

Florence Kelley (third from the left), chief factory inspector for the state of Illinois, fought tirelessly not only to regulate child labor, but also to secure a minimum wage for working women. She also served as president of the National Consumer's League to put pressure on the government to ban sweatshops.

In an 1881 essay on the distribution of wealth in France, French economist Paul Leroy-Beaulieu argued that reduced working hours gave workers more time for leisure and that living standards overall had improved. At the same time, he believed that the French should not sacrifice productivity for the sake of workers' free time. He worried that if workers were allowed more time off, other nations would begin to compete with French manufacturers. His argument showed that Leroy-Beaulieu was aware that a global industrial economy was in the making, but his views also suggest stereotypical racial thinking common in late nineteenth century about the sources of competition.

The thesis that the condition of the worker . . . has improved during the last quarter or half century, does not require any more proof . . . What can we say about his leisure? Is the worker of today a greater slave to his work than in the past? Is it the case that his more substantial and varied food, his cleaner and more spacious housing, his more comfortable and elegant furnishings . . . insurance against illness and sometimes against old age, the increase in personal savings, are all bought by a greater number of hours spent at work, by a greater sacrifice of his freedom and the time he could spend in relaxation, pursuing his hobbies . . . in the comfort of the family? . . . The evidence of the facts and figures enables us to give an unequivocal reply. The working day has been reduced to a level which makes it more humane. [Formerly] [w]orkers were completely dominated by their work, from daybreak until they went home to bed, and were allowed only a few moments respite . . . to attend to their physical needs . . . On Sundays only, and not even always then, the worker recovered the freedom which he had been without on the previous six days and unaccustomed to his freedom did not know how to use it. Who would dare to suggest that the situation is the same today? In the recent past, for we are referring to a situation which existed only 30 or 40 years ago, a working day of 14 or 15 hours was not unusual, both in home based as well as factory production. Nowadays the duration of work is not more than 12 hours, and even that is much too long. French law has fixed it at this figure; Swiss law has reduced it to 11 hours; in England it is down to 9 1/2 hours; in Paris and in nearly all the cities, in innumerable occupations it does not exceed 10; in the mines it is generally below this and in most of the factories it varies between 10 1/2 and 11 hours. Thus out of 24 hours a day the worker has 13 for his own needs

Fashionable men and women stroll along the Seine near Paris in 1884. The working-class man at the left, relaxing on the grass and smoking his pipe, contrasts with the stiff men and women holding parasols and shows how social classes sometimes mixed while enjoying leisure time in public parks.

and if we deduct sleep and meals, he has three or four hours to attend to his own affairs, for family life, amusements, conversation, and reading, in addition to having the whole of Sunday free. Contrary to what is often claimed, this can in no sense be regarded as slavery; and it is probable that soon, in the whole of Europe, the effective working day will be everywhere reduced to 10 hours, or to 60 hours out of the 168 in the week, not through legislation, but at the request of the parties concerned; deducting 9 hours per day for sleep and meals, the worker will be able to enjoy 45 hours per week. Any further improvements could only be achieved by incurring great disadvantages; there is a need to be on guard against the yellow race, the Chinese and the Japanese, without mentioning the Indian, who, when they possess our mechanical arts and industrial discoveries will perhaps show European workers and those in the United States, by a course of cruel lessons, the need for hard work, sobriety and temperance.

The facts that we have put together show quite clearly that all classes of the nation have participated in the general progress and that the working class has particularly benefited in the triple sense of an improvement in their material well being, an increase in security and the growth of leisure.

Afterword

The industrial revolution radically transformed society everywhere it occurred. It permanently altered the way people grow and cultivate food and produce and transport goods. It also made these goods available to more people. But historians have debated the positive and negative aspects of industrialization for years. Most agree that it produced tremendous wealth for middle-class employers at the top of society, but that it also threw into dramatic relief the gulf that separated rich from poor and accentuated the divisions between employers and workers. Indeed, industrialization had many negative effects on social life—poverty, unequal pay, and exploitation of workers. But the industrial revolution also had long-lasting positive effects.

A phenomenal number of new inventions and technical processes made the production of goods that ordinary people could afford more efficient and paved the way for mass consumption. The effects of these developments are still being felt today. Take clothing, for example. Before the industrial revolution, rich aristocrats and wealthy members of the middle class could buy their clothing ready-made (or made to order) from dressmakers and tailors. But this could be terribly expensive. Most ordinary working people made their clothing at home, stitching by hand (a job mostly women performed) by daylight or at night by the light of a candle. But the development of new machinery powered by steam in the early 1800s in England and the United States revolutionized clothing production. It made possible the production of huge amounts of cloth faster than ever before at cheaper prices. And beginning in the 1820s, clothing manufacturers in England and the United States hired large numbers of seamstresses and tailors to sew clothes to sell in stores. The invention of the sewing machine in the 1830s and its popularization in the 1850s and 1860s marked another revolution in garment manufacture. Seamstresses and tailors, working either in their own homes or in large garment workshops, turned out hundreds of shirts, suits, and dresses each week, feeding a growing market for mass-produced clothes.

The Eiffel Tower in Paris and the buildings around it glow with electric lights—a novelty at the end of the nineteenth century. The tower was completed in 1889, just in time for the International Exposition, which celebrated industrial achievements and economic progress.

Other processes born of the industrial revolution had equally long-lasting effects. The invention of new ways of processing iron made possible the building of railways and bridges that benefited middle and working classes alike. Railway building everywhere— in the United States, Europe, Russia, and Japan—allowed the rapid transportation of raw materials, finished goods, and people. In the 1840s, railway owners in England organized inexpensive day trips to the seaside so that workers in industrial cities could escape to the beach on Sunday. In fact, it was as a result of the industrial revolution that the weekend was born. Reformers, horrified at the poor conditions and long hours under which workers labored began to listen to their pleas for a day of rest, or as one writer called it, "the right to be lazy." Employers also began to see that rested workers were more productive and had fewer accidents. Gradually, and at different times in different countries, governments legislated a shorter workday and eventually a shorter work week.

Eventually, at least some of the enormous wealth created by industrialization filtered down to the workers whose labor produced it. Overall, workers' wages increased during the course of the nineteenth century, as the industrial revolution spread around the globe. Workers' living standards also improved as higher wages enabled them to eat a better diet and purchase more consumer goods, such as clothing and furniture. Middle-class reformers convinced municipalities to clean up industrial cities, and improvements in workers' housing also produced better living standards.

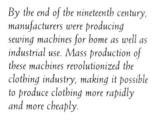

By the end of the nineteenth century, manufacturers were producing sewing machines for home as well as industrial use. Mass production of these machines revolutionized the clothing industry, making it possible to produce clothing more rapidly and more cheaply.

At the same time as they worked to shorten the workday and give birth to the weekend, reformers also paid attention to how workers spent their leisure time. They encouraged the building of public libraries, where workers could read and educate themselves, and the creation of urban parks, such as Central Park in New York and Hyde Park in London, where workers could walk, play, and breathe fresh air. Although reformers had a moral agenda, believing that libraries and parks would encourage workers to spend less time drinking in pubs and cafés, these amenities improved life for everyone.

Alongside the social inequalities, pollution, and poverty that the industrial revolution brought about, tangible benefits to society also emerged. The invention of new production processes, new means of transportation, rising living standards, and the expansion of leisure—not only for the middle class, but for workers as well—are just some of these benefits that transformed the lives of people all over the world and remain with us today.

The steamship passing under the Saltash Bridge in Cornwall, England, represented the enormous advances in transportation brought about by the industrial revolution. By the 1850s, steamships carried passengers and goods from the west of the country down to the bustling port of Plymouth, while trains rattled by on the bridge above.

Timeline

1733
Englishman John Kay invents the flying shuttle

1760s–1830s
Enclosure Acts in England permit landlords to enclose common land

1764
English inventor James Hargreaves invents the spinning jenny

1769
Richard Arkwright invents the water frame in England

1776
English inventor James Watt produces the first efficient steam engine, revolutionizing transportation and production of textiles, coal, and iron goods; French minister of finances Anne Robert Jacques Turgot issues a Royal Edict banning guilds; Scottish political economist Adam Smith publishes *The Wealth of Nations*

1779
Samuel Crompton combines the technology of the spinning jenny and the water frame in the "spinning mule"

1787
Edmund Cartwright invents the power loom

1790
American manufacturer Samuel Slater opens his first mill in Rhode Island

1799
English Combination Acts in Britain make it illegal for workers to unionize

1802
Health and Morals of Apprentices Act in Britain limits apprentices' labor to twelve hours a day

1807
British Parliament votes to abolish slave trade and United States forbids Southern planters to engage in slave trade

1811–1815
Luddite riots occur in England and France

1813
Francis Cabot Lowell builds his first cotton textile factory in Massachusetts

1815
George Stephenson builds the first steam locomotive in England

1819
First Factory Acts in Britain limit children's age of employment and working hours

1821
London Cooperative and Economical Society forms

1823
Lowell Mills open in Massachusetts

1824
British Combination Acts are repealed; women lead a strike at a textile mill in Pawtucket, Rhode Island

1829
Grand General Union of Operative Spinners forms in England

1833
British Parliamentary Commission investigates the labor of women and children in textile factories and limits the working hours of children and youths; Britain bans slavery throughout the British empire

1834
First strike of women mill workers in Lowell, Massachusetts, to protest a wage cut

1836
Major strike by Lowell millworkers

1838
Frenchman Louis-Jacques Mandé Daguerre discovers a way to chemically "fix" a photographic image

1845
Frederick Engels publishes his *Condition of the Working Class in England*

1847

British Parliament passes Ten Hours Bill, limiting women's and children's workday to ten hours; British Mines Act prohibits the employment of women and children underground in mines; New Hampshire passes the first ten-hours law in the United States

1848

Democratic revolutions occur all over Europe; middle class demands political rights; Karl Marx and Frederick Engels publish *The Communist Manifesto*

1851

Crystal Palace Exhibition in London displays industrial goods from around the world

1855

Englishman Henry Bessemer invents a process for refining and mass producing steel

1860s

Japanese industrialization begins; in United States, some states begin to pass eight-hour workday laws; individual states in the United States legislate the eight-hour day

1860

Massive strike by shoemakers for higher wages in Lynn, Massachusetts

1861

Englishwoman Isabella Beeton publishes *Mrs. Beeton's Book of Household Management*; emancipation of serfs in Russia

1864

International Working Men's Association forms

1866

Russian anarchist Mikhail Bakunin publishes his "Revolutionary Catechism"

1870s

Russia begins massive railway building, facilitates exploitation of coal and iron and encourages growth of cities

1870

French miners strike for higher wages and shorter hours at the Le Creusot mines in central France

1871

French transportation worker Eugene Pottier writes the words to "L'Internationale"; seventeen years later Pierre Degeyter sets the words to music

1874

French government outlaws women's and children's work in underground mines

1884

France legalizes labor unions

1885

Emile Zola publishes *Germinal* in France

1886

Haymarket riot and massacre in Chicago; American Federation of Labor founded

1888

London match girls strike to protest low wages and health hazards at work

1890

American journalist and photographer Jacob Riis publishes *How the Other Half Lives*

1891

Protest for eight-hour workday in Fourmies, France demonstrate results in ten deaths and eighty injured

1892–1916

Russians build the trans-Siberian railway

1903

Crimmitschau Workers' Strike in Germany protests low wages; National Women's Trade Union League is formed in the United States

1905

Vladimir Ilyich Lenin publishes *Imperialism: The Highest Stage of Capitalism*; International Workers of the World (IWW) founded in Chicago, Illinois

1909

Twenty thousand shirtwaist makers, most of them immigrant women, strike in New York City

1912

Twenty-five thousand textile workers strike in Lawrence, Massachusetts; police shoot one woman striker

1916

United States Congress outlaws child labor; Supreme Court judges law unconstitutional in 1918 and overturns it, then reinstates it in 1938

1919

French parliament mandates the eight-hour day for all workers

Further Reading

The Industrial Revolution

Berg, Maxine. *The Age of Manufactures, 1700–1820: Industry, Innovation, and Work in Britain.* New York: Routledge, 1994.

Cameron, Rondo E. *France and the Industrial Development of Europe.* Princeton, N.J.: Princeton University Press, 1968.

Cipolla, Carlo M., ed. *The Industrial Revolution, 1700–1914.* New York: Fontana, 1976.

Farr, James R., ed. *The Industrial Revolution in Europe, 1750–1914.* Detroit: Thomson, 2003.

Hindle, Brook, and Steven Lubar. *Engines of Changes: The American Industrial Revolution, 1790–1860.* Washington, D.C.: Smithsonian Institution, 1986.

Hobsbawm, Eric. *Industry and Empire.* Revised edition, revised and updated with Chris Wrigley. New York: Penguin, 1999.

Mokyr, Joel, ed. *The British Industrial Revolution: An Economic Perspective.* 2nd edition. Boulder: Westview Press, 1999.

More, Charles. *Understanding the Industrial Revolution.* New York: Routledge, 2000.

Mosk, Karl. *Japanese Industrial History: Technology, Urbanization, and Economic Growth.* Armonk, New York: M. E. Sharpe, 2001.

Reiber, Alfred J. *Merchants and Entrepreneurs in Imperial Russia.* Chapel Hill: University of North Carolina Press, 1982.

Stearns, Peter. *The Industrial Revolution and World History.* 2nd edition. Boulder: Westview Press, 1998.

Economics

Heilbroner, Robert L., ed. *Essential Adam Smith.* New York: W.W. Norton, 1986.

Moran, William. *The Belles of New England: The Women Of the Textile Mills and the Families Whose Wealth They Wove.* New York: St. Martin's, 2002.

Smith, Adam. *The Wealth of Nations.* New York: Modern Library, 2000.

Gender, Race, and Families

Blewett, Mary H. *Constant Turmoil: The Politics of Industrial Life in Nineteenth Century New England.* Amherst: University of Massachusetts Press, 2000.

Davidoff, Leonore, and Catherine Hall. *Family Fortunes: Men and Women of the English Middle Class, 1780–1850.* Chicago: University of Chicago Press, 1985.

Dublin, Thomas. *Women at Work: The Transformation of Work and Community in Lowell, Massachusetts, 1826–1860.* New York: Columbia University Press, 1979.

Dublin, Thomas, ed. *Farm to Factory: Women's Letters, 1830–1860.* New York: Columbia University Press, 1981.

Frader, Laura L., and Sonya O. Rose, eds. *Gender and Class in Modern Europe.* Ithaca, N.Y.: Cornell University Press, 1996.

Horn, Pamela. *Children's Work and Welfare, 1780–1890.* Cambridge: Cambridge University Press, 1995.

Horton, James Oliver, and Lois E. Horton. *Slavery and the Making of America.* New York: Oxford University Press, 2005.

Kessler-Harris, Alice. *Out to Work: A History of Wage-Earning Women in the United States.* New York: Oxford University Press, 1982.

Kirby, Peter. *Child Labour in Britain, 1750–1870.* New York: Palgrave Macmillan, 2003.

Kraus, Alisa C. *Every Child a Lion: The Origins of Maternal and Infant Health Policy in the United States and France, 1890–1920.* Ithaca, N.Y.: Cornell University Press, 1993.

Lewis, Jane, ed. *Protecting Women: Labor Legislation in Europe, the United States, and Australia, 1880–1920.* Urbana: University of Illinois Press, 1995.

Nardinelli, Clark. *Child Labor and the Industrial Revolution.* Bloomington: Indiana University Press, 1990.

Smith, Bonnie G. *Ladies of the Leisure Class.* Princeton, N.J.: Princeton University Press, 1981.

Tilly, Louise. *Industrialization and Gender Inequality.* Washington, D.C.: American Historical Association, 1993.

Tilly, Louise, and Joan W. Scott. *Women, Work, and Family.* New York: Routledge, 1989.

Valenze, Deborah. *The First Industrial Woman.* New York: Oxford University Press, 1995.

Zlotnick, Susan. *Women, Writing, and the Industrial Revolution.* Baltimore, Md.: Johns Hopkins University Press, 1998.

Technology and Innovation

Auerbach, Jeffrey. *The Great Exhibition of 1851: A Nation on Display.* New Haven, Conn.: Yale University Press, 1999.

Birdsall, Derek, and Carlo M. Cipolla. *The Technology of Man: A Visual History.* London: Wildwood House, 1980.

Bunch, Bryan H., with Alexander Hellemans. *The History of Science and Technology: A Browser's Guide to the Great*

Discoveries and Inventions and the People Who Make Them. Boston: Houghton Mifflin, 2004.

Cadbury, Deborah. *Dreams of Iron and Steel: Seven Wonders of the Nineteenth Century, from the Building of the London Sewers to the Panama Canal*. London: Fourth Estate, 2004.

Headrick, Daniel R. *The Tentacles of Progress: Technology Transfer in the Age of Imperialism, 1850–1940*. New York: Oxford University Press, 1988.

Hounshell, David. *From the American System to Mass Production, 1800–1932: The Development of Manufacturing Technology in the United States*. Baltimore, Md.: Johns Hopkins University Press, 1984.

Landes, David. *The Unbound Prometheus: Technological Change and Industrial Development in Western Europe from 1750 to the Present Day*. 2nd edition. Cambridge: Cambridge University Press, 2003.

Marsden, Ben. *Watt's Perfect Engine: Steam and the Age of Invention*. New York: Columbia University Press, 2002.

Mokyr, Joel. *The Lever of Riches: Technological Creativity and Economic Progress*. New York: Oxford University Press, 1990.

Social Histories

Daunton, Martin J. *Housing the Workers: 1850–1914: A Comparative Perspective*. London and New York: Leicester University Press, 1990.

Faler, Paul G. *Mechanics and Manufacturers in the Early Industrial Revolution: Lynn, Massachusetts, 1760–1860*. Albany: State University of New York Press, 1981.

Fitton, R. S. *The Arkwrights: Spinners of Fortune*. New York: St. Martin's, 1989.

Gutman, Herbert G. *Work, Culture, and Society in Industrializing America: Essays in American Working-Class and Social History*. New York: Knopf, 1976.

Halttunen, Karen. *Confidence Men and Painted Women: A Study of Middle-Class Culture in America, 1830–1870*. New Haven, Conn.: Yale University Press, 1982.

Laurie, Bruce, ed. *Artisans Into Workers: Labor in Nineteenth Century America*. New York: Hill and Wang, 1989.

Moch, Leslie Page. *Moving Europeans: Migration in Western Europe Since 1650*. 2nd edition. Bloomington: Indiana University Press, 2003.

Prude, Jonathan. *The Coming of Industrial Order: Town and Factory Life in Rural Massachusetts, 1810–1860*. New York: Cambridge University Press, 1983.

Riis, Jacob A. *How the Other Half Lives: Studies among the Tenements of New York*. New York: Penguin, 1997.

Rorabaugh, W. J. *The Craft Apprentice: From Franklin to the Machine Age in America*. New York: Oxford University Press, 1986.

Schofer, Lawrence. *The Formation of a Modern Labor Force: Upper Silesia, 1865-1914*. Berkeley: University of California Press, 1975.

Tucker, Barbara. *Samuel Slater and the Origins of the American Textile Industry, 1790–1860*. Ithaca, N.Y.: Cornell University Press, 1984.

Watson, Bruce. *Bread and Roses: Mills, Migrants, and the Struggle for the American Dream*. New York: Viking, 2005.

Workers and Protest

Arneson, Eric, Julie Greene, and Bruce Laurie, eds. *Labor Histories: Class, Politics, and the Working-Class Experience*. Urbana: University of Illinois Press, 1998.

Hobsbawm, Eric. *Workers: Worlds of Labor*. New York: Pantheon, 1984.

Perrot, Michele. *Workers on Strike in France, 1871–1890*. Translated by Chris Turner. New York: Berg, 1987.

Roediger, David, and Franklin Rosemont, eds. *Haymarket Scrapbook*. Chicago: C. H. Kerr, 1986.

Thompson, Edward P. *The Making of the English Working Class*. London: Penguin, 1963.

Biographies

Pascal, Janet. *Jacob Riis: Reporter and Reformer*. New York: Oxford University Press, 2005.

Smith, Roy C. *Adam Smith and the Origins of American Enterprise: How America's Industrial Success Was Forged by the Timely Ideas of a Brilliant Scots Economist*. New York: St. Martin's, 2004.

Novels

Dickens, Charles. *Hard Times*. New York: Norton, 1990.

Gaskell, Elizabeth. *Mary Barton*. New York: Knopf, 1994.

Gaskell, Elizabeth. *North and South*. New York and London: Penguin, 1983.

Zola, Emile. *Germinal*. Translated by Roger Pearson. New York and London: Penguin, 2004.

Zola, Emile. *The Ladies' Paradise*. Berkeley: University of California Press, 1993.

Websites

Annie Besant and the London 1888 Match Girls Strike
http://anglais.u-paris10.fr/
article.php3?id_article=84

This site provides a review of the match girls strike and includes images of the strikers as well as links to other examples of British working-class protest movements.

Blacknet
www.blacknet.co.uk/history/index.html

This website examines the black presence in Britain and notably the migration of Africans to eighteenth- and nineteenty-century Britain during the period of the Atlantic slave trade and the industrial revolution.

Eco-museum of Fourmis-Trelon, France
www.theotherside.co.uk/tmheritage/
visit/visit-avesnes-ecomusee.htm

The website of this eco-museum introduces one of the regions where the industrial revolution began in eighteenth- and nineteenth-century France, offering information about the region's textile production, iron smelting, forging of iron tools, and glass making.

History of International Migration
www.let.leidenuniv.nl/history/migration/
chapter3.html

Sponsored by Leiden University in the Netherlands, this site contains useful information about how the industrial revolution stimulated the movement of peoples across Europe and between Europe and America. Also included are links to information on Irish migration.

Ironbridge Gorge Museums
www.ironbridge.org.uk/

The website of this English museum offers a virtual tour of the first iron bridge in the world and the surrounding industrial towns. Visitors can view the inventions of Abraham Darby and the products that were made in the Ironbridge Gorge.

John Bull and Uncle Sam: Four Centuries of British-American Relations
www.loc.gov/exhibits/british/brit-5.html

This Library of Congress online exhibit features information about some of the principal inventions used during the industrial revolution on both sides of the Atlantic, such as the steam engine, locomotive, and electromagnet.

Lowell National Historical Park
www.nps.gov/lowe/loweweb/
Lowell_History/prologue.htm

The website of Lowell National Historical Park in Lowell, Massachusetts—one of the birthplaces of America's industrial revolution—tells about nineteenth-century industry in Lowell: how textiles were made, the lives and working conditions of "mill girls," and the use of waterpower in early industry.

Saugus Iron Works
www.nps.gov/sair/

The Saugus Iron Works in Massachusetts was the first in the United States to incorporate all aspects of the iron-making process. The National Park Service website features explanations of iron-making technology as well as the role of iron in early Massachusetts.

The Union Makes Us Strong: Trade Union Council History Online
http://tuc1.unl.ac.uk/index.php

The site of the British Trades Union Council contains information on the history of trade unions in Britain, including its prominent leaders, interactive timelines, and images.

Victoria Station: the Great Exhibition at the Crystal Palace
www.victorianstation.com/palace.html

An illustrated introduction to Britain's celebration of the industrial and economic achievements of Britain's industrial revolution, held in London in 1851.

Victorian Poor Law and Life in the Workhouse
www.victorianweb.org/history/poorlaw/
poorlawov.html

Created by a professor at Brown University, this site includes descriptions of the ways the British dealt with the poverty of the industrial revolution. It also provides images of the Rotherham and Southwell workhouses and descriptions of the workhouses by contemporary writers.

Text Credits

Every effort has been made to contact and secure permission to reproduce the documents in this book from the original copyright holder.

Main Text

p. 11: Norbert Truquin, "Memoirs and Adventures of a Proletarian in Times of Revolution," in *The French Worker: Autobiographies from the Early Industrial Era*, ed. and trans. Mark Traugott (Berkeley: University of California Press, 1993), 254.

pp. 22–23: Laurel Thatcher Ulrich, *A Midwife's Tale: The Life of Martha Ballard Based on Her Diary, 1785–1812* (New York: Vintage, 1991), 36–38. From A MIDWIFE'S TALE by Laurel Thatcher Ulrich, copyright © 1990 by Laurel Thatcher Ulrich. Used by permission of Alfred A. Knopf, a division of Random House, Inc.

p. 24: Report by Wintgens to v. Buggenhagen on the woolen industry in Aachen, Duisberg, February 8, 1781. Printed in Horst Krüger, *Geschicte der Manufacturen und der manufacturarbeiter in Preussen* (Berlin, 1958), 508–10, cited in Sidney Pollard and Colin Holmes, eds., *Documents of European Economic History*, vol. 1, *The Process of Industrialization, 1750–1870* (New York: St. Martin's Press, 1968) 88–89. Reproduced with permission of Palgrave Macmillan.

pp. 25–26: Peter Gaskell, *Artisans and Machinery*, (London: John W. Parker, 1836), 6, 11–16.

pp. 26–27: "Poem Descriptive of the Manners of the Clothiers," written about the year 1730, cited by Edward Thompson, *The Making of the English Working Class* (Harmondsworth: Penguin, 1963), 300–301, bracketed translations by L. L. Frader. Thompson's footnote says: "The M.S. copy in Leeds Reference Library is transcribed by F. B. in The Publications of the Thorseby Society XLI Part 3 No. 95, 1947, pp. 275–9; there are extracts in H. Heaton, Yorkshire Woollen and Worsted Industries (1920), 344–7."

pp. 28–30: Regulations relating to the gild of locksmiths, gun and watch and spring makers, Bandenburg, Prussia, 1734. Printed in C. O. Mylius, *Corpus Constitutionum Marchicarum*, 5 vols. (1737–40), vol. 5, part 2, appendix, pp. 61–63, cited in Pollard and Holmes, *The Process of Industrialization*, 43–45.

pp, 30–31: Edict of 1776. Printed in Robert Jacques Turgot, *Oeuvres . . . avec les notes de Dupont de Nemours* 2nd ed., vol. 2 (Paris, 1884), 302–7, cited in Pollard and Holmes, *The Process of Industrialization*, 53–55.

p. 32: "Pétition des femmes du Tiers-Etat au Roi, 1er janvier 1789" (n.p., n.d.) in Bibliothèque historique de la Ville de Paris, 12807, vol. 1, no. 17. Translated by and reproduced in Darlene Gay Levy, Harriet Branson Applewhite, and Mary Durham Johnson, *Women of Revolutionary Paris, 1789–1795* (Urbana: University of Illinois Press, 1979), 18–20.

pp. 33–34: Frances Collier, *The Family Economy of the Working Classes in the Cotton Industry, 1784–1833*, ed. R. S. Fitton (New York: Augustus M. Kelley, 1968), 55.

pp. 34–35: William Coxe, *Travels into Poland, Russia, Sweden and Denmark*, 5 vols. (London, 1784; 4th ed. 1792) 3:174–81, quoted in Pollard and Holmes, *The Process of Industrialization*, 24–25.

pp. 35–37: Rev. D. Davies, "The case of the Labourers in Husbandry" (1795), pp. 55–57, cited in G. D. H. Cole and A. W. Filson, eds., *British Working-Class Movements: Select Documents, 1789–1875* (London: MacMillan, 1951), 3–4.

pp. 37–38: J. G. Elsner, *Landwirtschaftliche Reise durch Schlesien*, 4 vols., in 2 (Breslau 1823) vols. 1–2, vol. I, pp. 70–74, cited in Pollard and Holmes, eds. and trans., *The Process of Industrialization*, 261–63.

p. 39: Arthur Young, *A Tour in Ireland: with general observations on the present state of that kingdom, made in the years 1776, 1777, and 1778 and brought down to the end of 1779*, vol. 1 (Dublin: G Bonham for Whitestone, 1780), 384–87.

p. 44: Adam Smith, *An Inquiry into the Nature and Causes of the Wealth of Nations*, ed. Kathryn Sutherland (New York: Oxford University Press, 1993), 291–92, 299.

pp. 44–45: Samuel Smiles, *Self Help: Character and Conduct* (London: John Murray, 1859), 2, 8, 21, 23, 238–39.

pp. 46–48: *The Family Economy, 14–15*.

pp. 48: Charles Dickens, *Hard Times* (1843; reprint, New York: W. W. Norton, 1990), 56.

pp. 49–50: Andrew Ure, *The Philosophy of Manufactures*, 3rd ed. (1835) (New York: Burt Franklin, 1861), 29, 339–40.

pp. 52: Richard Guest, *Compendious History of the Cotton Manufacture* (Manchester, 1823), 44–48, cited in Brian Tierney and Joan Scott, eds., *Western Societies: A Documentary History* vol. 2 (New York: Knopf, 1984), 140–43.

pp. 52–53: B. Samuelson, Esq., M.P. to the Vice-President of the Committee of Council on Education, 1867, *British Parliamentary Papers, 1867–1868*, vol. 54, 27–31; reproduced in Pollard and Holmes, *Industrial Power and National Rivalry*, 88–89.

pp. 53–55: Solomon Northup, *Narratives of Solomon Northup, Twelve Years A Slave . . .* (Auburn, New York: Derby and Miller, 1853), 165–69.

pp. 55–57: Betina Eisler, *The Lowell Offering: Writings by New England Mill Women* (New York: Harper, 1977), 51–53.

p. 57: Louis Reybaud, *Etudes sur le régime des manufactures: Condition des ourvriers en soie* (Paris: Michel Lévy Frères, 1859), 38–39, trans. L. L. Frader.

pp. 58–60: Schroterand Becker, ed. *Die deutsche Maschinenbau-industrie*, 112–16, cited in Pollard and Holmes, eds. and trans., *The Process of Industrialization*, 534–36.

pp. 60–62: William Cobbett, *Political Register*, November 20, 1824, vol. 2, cited in Richard L. Tames, *Documents of the Industrial Revolution, 1750–1850* (London: Hutchinson Educational, 1971), 91–92.

pp. 62–65: Emile Zola, *Germinal*, trans. Peter Collier (New York: Oxford University Press, 1993), 41–43. By permission of Oxford University Press.

pp. 76–77: John Ruskin, "Of Queen's Gardens," in *Sesame and Lilies* [1865] (New York: John Wiley and Son's, 1880), 90–92.

pp. 77–78: Reverend Rufus Wm. Bailey, *The Family Preacher or Domestic Duties* (New York: John S. Taylor, 1837), 22–25, 34.

pp. 78–79: Isabella Beeton, *Mrs. Beeton's Book of Household Management* [1861] (London, 1880), iii, 1–2, 5–8, 21–22, excerpted from Erna Olafson Hellerstein, Leslie Parker Hume, and Karen M. Offen, eds., *Victorian Women: A Documentary Account of Women's Lives in Nineteenth-Century England, France, and the United States* (Stanford: Stanford University Press, 1981), 296–301.

pp. 81–83: Lydia Maria Child Papers, Anti-Slavery Collection, Cornell University Library, Ithaca, N.Y., cited in Gerda Lerner, *The Female Experience: An American Documentary* (Indianapolis: Bobbs-Merrill, 1979), 125–26.

pp. 83–84: A. Guépin, *Nantes au XIXe siècle* (Nantes, 1835), cited in Pollard and Holmes, eds. and trans., *The Process of Industrialization*, 494–96.

pp. 85–86: Alexander Schneer, *Über die Zustände der arbeitenden Klassen in Breslau*, (Berlin, 1845), 25–31, in Pollard and Holmes, *The Process of Industrialization*, 497–500.

pp. 87–88: *Parliamentary Papers, 1833*, vol. 20, Factories Inquiry Commission, *First Report of the Central Board*, C. 1, 42–43.

pp. 88–90: Gaskell, *The Manufacturing Population of England* (London: Baldwin and Cradock, 1833), 106–9.

pp. 91–92: *Parliamentary Papers, 1843*, vol. 14, *Children's Employment Commission*, part 1, 45, 61–62, cited in Hellerstein, Hume, and Offen, *Victorian Women*, 236–37.

pp. 92–93: Adolphe-Jean Focillon, "Tailleur d'habits de Paris," in Frédéric Le Play, *Les Ouvriers européens*, vol 6, *Les Ouvriers de l'occident, populations desorganisées*, 2nd ed. (Paris: A. Mame et Files, 1878), pp. 387–414, trans. Laura L. Frader.

pp. 94–95: Frederick Engels, *The Condition of the Working Class in England*, with an introduction by Eric Hobsbawm (London: Panther Books-Granada Publishing, 1969), 172–75.

pp. 100–103: Nelly Hoyt and Thomas Cassirer, eds. and trans., *Encyclopedia: Selections [by] Diderot, d'Alembert, and a Society of Men of Letters* (New York: Bobbs-Merrill Co., 1965), 259–62, 266–267.

pp. 103–104: Charles Mackenzie, *Facts Relative to the Present State of the British Cotton Colonies*, 56–57.

pp. 104–105: Charles Mackenzie, *Facts Relative to the Present State of the British Cotton Colonies and to the Connection of their Interests with those of the Mother Country* (Edinburgh: Thomas Bryce and Co., 1811), 13, 15, 16, 19–20.

pp. 105–106: From Speeches to the Reichstag. Printed in Heinrich von Poschinger, *Fürst Bismarck als Volkswirth* vol. 3, (Berlin 1889–1891), 14–15, 86–89, 209–10, cited in Pollard and Holmes, eds. and trans., *Documents of European Economic History*, vol. 2, *Industrial Power and National Rivalry, 1870–1914* (New York: St. Martin's Press, 1972), 172–74.

pp. 106–107: Jules Ferry, *Le Tonkin et la Mere Patrie* (Paris, 1890), 37, 40–43. Printed in G. Mosse et al., eds., *Europe in Review* (Chicago, 1964), 369–70, and in Pollard and Holmes, *Industrial Power and National Rivalry*, 169–70.

pp. 108–109: Henry Cooke, (British Commercial Agent in Russia), *Report on Russian Railways*, Diplomatic and Consular Reports, Miscellaneous Series, no. 522, (March 1900), 4–7, cited in Pollard and Holmes, *Industrial Power and National Rivalry*, 134–35.

pp. 109–10: S. I. Kanatchikov, *Iz istorii moego bytiia* (The Story of My Life) (Moscow, and Leningrad, 1929), in Victoria E. Bonnell, ed., *The Russian Worker: Life and Labor under the Tsarist Regime* (Berkeley: University of California Press, 1983), 45–47.

pp. 110–11: J. J. Rein, *The Industries of Japan Together with an Account of its Agriculture, Forestry, Arts, and Commerce* (London: Hodder and Stoughton, 1889; facsimile edition published by Curzon Press, St. John's Studios, Church Road, Richmond, Surrey TW9 2QA), 380–81.

p. 116: Letter to a Huddersfield employer, 1812. Home Office Papers, 40/41, cited in Cole and Filson, *British Working-Class Movements*, 114–15.

pp. 117–18: *The Economist*, March 2, 1822, cited in Cole and Filson, *British Working-Class Movements*, 207–9.

pp. 119–20: Cole and Filson, *British Working-Class Movements*

p. 121: Home Office Papers, (1829), cited in Cole and Filson, *British Working-Class Movements,*, 247–51.

pp. 122–123: Louis Blanc, *The Organization of Labor*, (1840), translated by Marie Paula Dickoré in University of Cincinnati Studies, series 2, vol. 7, no. 1 (January–February, 1911) , 15–16, 51–56.

pp. 123–25: Karl Marx and Frederick Engels, *The Communist Manifesto*, with an introduction and notes by A. J. P. Taylor (Harmondsworth, England: Penguin, 1985), 80–91.

pp. 125–26: Cole and Filson, *British Working-Class Movements*, 527–28.

pp. 126–27: "The Internationale," in *Rebel Voices: An IWW Anthology*, ed. Joyce L. Kornbluh (Ann Arbor: University of Michigan Press, 1964), 174.

pp. 127–28: Mikhail Bakunin, "Revolutionary Catechism," in *Bakunin on Anarchy: Selected Works by the Activist-Founder of World Anarchism*, ed. Sam Dolgoff (New York: Knopf, 1972), 76–81.

pp. 129–30: "Compte rendu de J. Card," Session of September 7, 1866, *La Première Internationale: Receuil de documents*, ed. Jacques Freymond (Geneva: Librairie Droz, 1962), 1: 75–6, trans. Laura L. Frader.

pp. 130–31: Paule Minck, "Le Travail des Femmes: discours prononcé par Mme. Paule Minck à la réunion publique du Vauxhall, le 13 juillet 1868," (Paris: Imprimerie A. Levy, 1868) in *Paule Minck: Communard et féministe*, preface et commentaries d'Alain Dalote (Paris: Syros, 1981), 119–23, 128–29, trans. Laura L. Frader.

pp. 131–32: *The Jackson [Mississippi] Daily Clarion*, June 24, 1866, printed in Philip S. Foner and Ronald L. Lewis, eds., *Black Workers: A Documentary History from Colonial Times to the Present* (Philadelphia: Temple University Press, 1989), 142.

pp. 132–33: Leaflet printed in *Dokumente und Materialien zur Geschichte der deutschen Arbeiter-bewegung*, (Zentralkomite d. S.E.D., Berlin) series 1, vol. 4 (1967), pp. 91–95, cited in Pollard and Holmes, eds. and trans., *Industrial Power and National Rivalry: Documents of European Economic History*, vol. 2. (New York: St. Martin's Press, 1972), 352–55.

pp. 134–35: Elizabeth Gurley Flynn, "The Lawrence Textile Strike," in *The Rebel Girl* (New York: International Publishers, 1973), 127–28, 137–38.

pp, 136–37: Speech delivered by Michael Thomas Sadler, M.P. in the House of Commons, March 16, 1832. Reprinted in *Memoirs of the Life and Writing of Michael Thomas Sadler* (1842), 338–39, excerpted in Pike, "Hard Times," 117–18.

pp. 137–38: Massachusetts General Court, House of Representatives, House Document 50, (1845), 15–17, cited in Philip S. Foner, *The Factory Girls* (Chicago: University of Illinois Press, 1977), 241–42.

p. 139: "Report of Florence Kelley," in Illinois, Factory Inspectors, *Second Annual Report for the Year Ending December 15, 1894* (Springfield, Illinois, 1895), 12–24, cited in Robert H. Bremner, ed., *Children and Youth in America: A Documentary History*, vol. 2, 1866–1932 (Cambridge: Harvard University Press, 1971), 673.

pp. 140–41: Paul Leroy-Beaulieu, *Essai sur la répartition des richesses et sur la tendance à une moindre inégalité des conditions* (Paris, 1881), 42–44, trans. L. L. Frader.

Sidebars

p. 26: James Orr, "The Penitent," James Orr, *The Posthumous Works of James Orr of Ballycarry, with a Sketch of His Life* (Belfast: Francis D. Finlay, 1817), quoted by Jane Gray, "Gender and Uneven Working-class Formation in the Irish Linen Industry," in Laura L. Frader and Sonya O. Rose, eds., *Gender and Class in Modern Europe* (Ithaca: Cornell University Press, 1996), 37–38. © 1996 by Cornell University. Used by permission of the publisher, Cornell University Press.

p. 43: Richard L. Tames, ed., *Documents of the Industrial Revolution, 1750–1850* (London: Hutchinson Educational, 1971), 70.

p. 48: Adam Smith, *The Wealth of Nations*, ed. Andrew Skinner (Harmondsworth: Penguin, 1974), 109–12.

p. 58: Edward Baines, *History of the Cotton Manufacture in Great Britain* (1835), cited in Tames, *Documents of the Industrial Revolution*, 68. Employee, Marshall's Flax Mill, 1819, quoted in Tames, *Documents of the Industrial Revolution*, 93.

p. 86: Jacob Riis, *How the Other Half Lives: Studies Among the Tenements of New York*, ed. David Leviatin (Bedford St. Martin's, 1996), 141–42.

p. 88: *Parliamentary Papers*, 1842, vol. 17, 163, cited in Edgar Royston Pike, "Hard Times": Human Documents of the Industrial Revolution (New York: Praeger, 1966), 258

p. 91: R. A. Slaney, MP, reporting on the state of Birmingham, etc. State of Large Towns, 2nd Report, *Parliamentary Papers, 1845*, vol. 18, app., p. 18, cited in Pike, "Hard Times," 241–42.

p. 92: Lady Bell (Mrs. Hugh Bell), *At the Works: A Study of a Manufacturing Town* (1907 (London: Thomas Nelson and Sons, 1911), 123–24.

p. 94: Jemima Sanborn to Richard and Ruth Bennett, May 14, 1843, in *Farm to Factory: Women's Letters, 1830–1860* ed. Thomas Dublin (New York: Columbia, 1981), 25.

p. 99: Interview with Carl Lund, cited by Maths Isacson and Lars Magnusson, *Proto-Industrialization in Scandinavia: Craft Skills in the Industrial Revolution* (Leamington Spa: Berg, 1987), 132. The interview was cited in an exhibition, listed in the bibliography as *Verkstadsminnen*, (Stockholm: M. Rhenberg, 1953).

p. 105: V. I. Lenin, *Imperialism: The Highest Stage of Capitalism* (New York: International Publishers, 1905).

p. 106: Paul Leroy-Beaulieu, *De la colonisation chez les peuples modernes*, 4th edition (Paris: 1891).

p. 110: E. A. Oliunina, *Portnovskii promysel v Moskve I v derevniakh Moscovskoi I Riazanskoi gubernii: Materialy k istorii domashnei promysblennosti v Rossii* (Mosow, 1914), in Bonnell, *The Russian Worker*, 174.

p. 119: Harriet Hanson Robinson, *Loom and Spindle, or Life Among the Early Mill Girls* (New York: Crowell, 1898), 84–85.

p. 121: Opening Circular of the Metropolitan Trades' Union, from *Penny Papers for the People*, March 26, 1831, in Cole and Filson, *British Working Class Movements: Select Documents 1789–1875*, 246.

p. 130: Edward O'Donnell, "Women as Bread Winners: The Error of the Age," *The American Federationist* 4 (October 1897): 8.

Picture Credits

Index

Acknowledgments

The author thanks Rachel Gillett and Robyn Christensen for their invaluable assistance on this project.

About the Author

Laura L. Frader is professor of history and chair of the department of history at Northeastern University, and a faculty associate in residence at the Center for European Studies at Harvard University. Frader is the co-editor of *Gender and Class in Modern Europe* and author of *Peasants and Protest: Agricultural Workers, Politics and Unions in the Aude, 1850–1914*, and *Masculin/Féminin: Bodies, Citizens, and Breadwinners in Modern France*.